Published by

The Naval & Military Press Ltd

Unit 5 Riverside, Brambleside
Bellbrook Industrial Estate
Uckfield, East Sussex
TN22 1QQ England

Tel: +44 (0)1825 749494

www.naval-military-press.com
www.nmarchive.com

This guide-book has been prepared in a new and practical form to enable tourists to visit the war regions under the best possible conditions.

These regions have been divided into 17 sectors, as far as possible corresponding to the scenes of the various battles or natural regions. The tourist who wishes to cover one or other of these sectors, to follow a practical route, or discover the best hotel at which to stay, will find an index to this information on the first page of the " War regions " section, page 29.

The routes have been arranged in such a way as to allow the tourist to visit all interesting points without circuitous ways or loss of time. One day will suffice to visit each of the sectors 1, 2, 12, 13, 14, and from thence back to Paris.

The visit to the sectors 3, 4, 5, 7, and 8 may be performed in the same way to and from Nancy ; that of the sectors 10, 11, 15, 16, 17, from and back to Lille.

The visit to sector 6 (Alsace) contemplated in the route from Belfort may also be performed from Nancy.

The visit to sector 9 (Belgium) will take at least two days. Our hotel lists have been compiled only after careful inquiry as to their merits and comfort. The tourist may in all confidence apply there, and will certainly find good cuisine and accommodation.

Blue Section   -   **T H E   M O T O R I S T**
White Section   -   **THE GOODRICH TYRE**
Red Section   -   **THE   WAR   REGIONS**

The Motorist on the road

*W*E are here giving the Motorist all necessary *and useful information for his travelling, and practical advice for his general well-being.*

INDEX

The Motorist on his Journey

We think it indispensable to recall here both the various regulations to which every motorist has to submit if he wishes to avoid annoyance and the precautions we invite him to take in order to secure comfort on his journey.

Documents to be secured before starting

First of all, the motorist must be provided with the PINK CARD which is the *Driving License* and with the GREY CARD or *Free Pass*.

Moreover, he should carry with him his personal papers : Military pass, identity card, etc.

Below are the formalities to be complied with in case the motorist has not these documents.

We presume the driver, owner or chauffeur has his driving license (pink card).

In order to get the grey card it is sufficient to ask for it on 1-franc stamped paper at the Préfecture de Police (Head office of the Paris Police) if the driver resides in Paris, or at the Préfecture of the Department (County Préfecture) if he resides in the provinces. It is necessary to add to this application the certificate of the Mining Services which is supplied by the maker, or the grey card issued in the name of the car's seller (in the case of a second-hand car).

The official demand on stamped paper will have to be legalised by the Mayor or by the Commissary of Police.

If the car is of a current well-known type the grey card is delivered within a few days. If the car has no trade-mark or has a foreign little-known trade-mark, the Préfecture may call together the owner with the Mining Engineer in charge of the examination of cars.

Foreigners without an *International Free Pass* require to get a free pass from the departmental Mining Service of their choice.

||||||||||||||||||||||||||||||||||||||||||||||||||||||||||||||||||||||||||||||||||||||||||||||||||||||||||||||||||||

What we have said is sufficient only *if the car remains in France :* foreigners should also have their Permis de Séjour (license necessary for those living in France).

In order to go to ALSACE-LORRAINE obtain from the Paris Préfecture de Police, or from any departmental Préfecture in the Province, a *Safe-conduct* in the name of the driver and of each passenger ; each person having also to carry identity papers.

In order to go into the OCCUPIED ZONE or into BELGIUM, each person must have a passport issued by the Préfecture.

When this guide-book is published, possibly the passport formalities will be abolished or at any rate simplified.

How the Car must be equipped before starting

It must be provided with :

1. Its TWO IDENTITY PLATES according to regulations, the one bearing the name and address of the owner, the other the name of the maker, the specification of the car's type and its number in the series of manufacturing.

2. A FRONT AND REAR-PLATE showing the REGISTRATION NUMBER already entered on the grey card.

The figures, letters and dashes composing the Registration number must be painted white on black plates.

The standard sizes are 100 m/m (roughly 4 ins.) height of front-plate and 120 m/m (roughly 5 ins.) for the rear-plate. Letters and figures to measure 75 m/m (about 3 ins.) by 45 m/m (1¾ ins.) for the front and 100 m/m (4 ins.) by 60 m/m (2¼ ins.) for the rear ; dash 45 m/m (1¾ ins.) by 12 m/m (¼ in.) ; free space 30 m/m (1¼ ins.) ; front-plate 60 m/m (2½ ins.) by 15 m/m (⅗ ins.) and space 35 m/m (1½ ins.) on rear-plate.

Should the rear-plate be pierced the free space might be reduced to 20 m/m (⅘ in.) and the length of dash to 40 m/m (1¾ ins.).

If desired, the number may be written on two lines, the figures above and the letters below.

The regulations require the two plates to make one body with the frame or the carriage, or at least to be riveted.

3. At night AT LEAST TWO LAMPS ON THE FRONT ARE NECESSARY, a white and a green one. It is permitted to use strong searchlights, but blinding or dazzling lights are strictly forbidden.

At the rear the car must have a RED lamp and the rear-plate must be sufficiently illuminated.

In order to complete the equipment the car must be provided with good spare tyres wrapped in sheath, and a good reserve store of petrol.

It is advisable here to remind the motorist that between the pleasure and the discomfort of a tour there is sometimes only the thickness of a tyre.

The best security against breakdowns or accidents is to equip the car with Goodrich Safety Tread Tyres, which have been rightly named "The master of the road." Their endurance and non-skid qualities are equally remarkable.

But the best tyre will only give the maximum of satisfaction if it is used properly, chiefly with regard to limit of load and correct inflation.

On page 22 the tourist will find precise instructions on this subject which will save him much disagreeable expense and disappointment.

Starting

The chauffeur should fill up his tank with petrol, oil, and water. He should not forget the necessary repair tools, and should take with him a good section map.

Our road maps aim only at showing tourists the main roads, enabling them to visit places of interest in each sector without useless detours.

Do not forget to carry a camera, field-glasses, and a fountain pen.

It is indispensable also to possess cloaks, waterproofs and blankets for the breakdown emergencies in regions destitute of accommodation.

Road Regulations in France

Up till a short time ago the motorist in France was not favourably received by the general public.

Even if his reception is better to-day he risks meeting some evilly disposed people occasionally, and for this reason we recommend him to observe the road regulation strictly and to follow the advice we are giving him here.

You must constantly be master of your car at all speeds, and must be able to slow down to walking pace and stop immediately if necessary. The highest regulation speed is : 12½ miles per hour in a crowded place and 19 miles per hour in the open country.

You must follow the police regulations of every Department, and very often of each town you pass through.

Announce your approach by sounding your horn sufficiently.

Never leave your car without having first cut off the engine and blocked the brakes.

Keep always to your right sufficiently to allow a faster car to pass.

When crossing *keep to your right* and slow down as much as possible.

To pass to the left, sound your horn continuously and wait till there is room, but never attempt it in a *sharp turn of the road* or *on top of a hill, and always make sure that the road is clear.*

At sharp turns slow down as much as is necessary, and blow your horn sufficiently.

Slow down on top of a hill or at *crossing* of routes.

At a road crossing, should two cars arrive at the same time, *the car on the right* passes first, and if there is any danger of *collision*, both perform *a turn to the right.*

Slow down to regulation speed (8 miles) in each town and village you pass through, so that you can stop within 30 ft. on the road and 9 ft. on the street and blow your horn to announce your presence, even in the neighbourhood of an isolated house.

When approaching men or animals blow your horn, slow down, and stop if necessary.

Infringements

You are in fault :

If you are found without the pink and the grey cards.

If you keep the left of the road.

If your light is not sufficient.

If you have blinding or dazzling searchlights.

If the identity plates are not according to regulations.

If you have no Registration plates or if the rear-plate is not illumined.

If you let your motor smoke.

If you exceed speed limits.

If you do not obey all regulations of the places or regions *en route.*

In case of infringements :

You receive a warning first, then a legal document requesting you to appear before the police court. Never fail to go yourself or send a representative with your authorisation on 1-franc stamped paper.

If in the wrong, own it and apologise ; if you fear the affair may become serious consult a solicitor.

Official reports are admitted as evidence in the Courts, and the policemen's reports and the evidence of the passers-by as proofs.

In case of accident

Do not motor off, you will only be more severely condemned. Carry urgent help to the victims, and then gather all possible proofs and collect all details of the accident and all estimates of damage resulting from it. If possible let the damage be proved by an expert.

Should you yourself be the victim of the accident act in the same way.

It is always better to try to arrange matters peacefully, but if you have to appear before a Court take all necessary precautions, including the help of a solicitor.

See that you are permanently insured against all risks.

Railway Transportation Rules

If the car is injured and cannot be moved or if for any other reason it requires to be conveyed by railway :

You have the choice between the Grand Vitesse and the Petite Vitesse, with rates to correspond. The former is known as the " general tariff," and the latter as " No. 128 tariff."

Here is the method of procedure :

Communicate with the stationmaster of the nearest station, asking him to reserve a truck for you, and giving him the following particulars : Type and approximate weight of car, station to which the car is to be conveyed, the Department in which that station is, and whether that station has a siding in which the truck may be kept till your arrival.

Specify on the forwarding declaration form the weight and wheel base of car, also approximate mileage of the journey for guidance in arriving at the cost of carriage, and, in addition. mention the parts and accessories the car contains and certify that the tanks are empty.

Do not leave the magneto with your car.

If you do not cover your car with tarpaulin it will travel exposed, unless you have previously arranged for a covered van.

The companies are responsible only for the articles mentioned in the specification.

In cases of loss or damage let the loss or damage be confirmed by the stationmaster or his clerk on the consignment note or on the receipt, then claim against the company, within three days, by registered letter, or through an usher.

In case of a dispute between you and the company's clerks, do not argue the case, but take it up yourself and make your claim in writing within three days.

In case you fear litigation, refuse to accept delivery, and demand the services of a lawyer from the magistrate or Tribunal of Commerce.

The car must be removed within twenty-four hours of receipt of the company's advice note, provided it has been received before six o'clock. If not, the warehouse charge will be 1 franc per car per twenty-four hours.

8

At the Hotel

We have thought it advisable to print a list of the good hotels catering for Motorists in the principal towns in each of the War areas.

One must foresee the situation when these hotels will be full. The tourist may think that with his car he has every resource he requires: that he can easily find a good bed and meal at the nearest village, and some coach-house or shed to shelter his car.

It may not be easy to secure these, but it will always be possible, and the endeavour will not be the least interesting part of the trip. The tourist is assured beforehand of finding an excellent welcome from these honest inhabitants who have been for five years accustomed to give hospitality.

SAFETY

Self - preservation, the first law—operated as powerfully in the stone age as to-day and generally with barbaric effect --being the primal impulse of Egoism.

The preservation of *others* is a law of later growth and greater value—the product of civilisation.

When motoring, not only your own or even your passengers' safety, but that of other motorists and all users of the high road is the plain, civilised duty of civilised man, and no precaution is too great to secure it.

Now, as to skidding—some motorists, in their search for the ideal non-skid tyre, have to tediously weed out a dozen undesirable types—an expensive process and not without risk. Others, more fortunate, find it at once. The result is the same—once found, they finally adopt

GOODRICH · TYRES

BEST IN THE LONG RUN

11

GOOD

THE GOODRICH FACTORY, AKRON, OHIO

Established 50 years. It now covers an area of 120 acres, employs 25,000 people, and operates a capital of £25,000,000. It is the largest rubber installation in the world exclusively devoted to the manufacture of highest grade goods.

RICH

The works of the Société Française B. F. GOODRICH, 221 Boulevard
de Valmy, at Colombes, though not so extensive as those of the parent
factory at AKRON, OHIO, have been established on the same efficient
basis, and produce goods of an equally superior make.
(Retail Establishment : 38 bis Avenue de la Grande Armée, Paris.)

Products of GOODRICH Factory
at Colombes.

SPEED

Speed is not merely the privilege of racing experts or reckless drivers but the legacy of every man who knows how to get the best results out of his car.

Whether you drive six cylinders or twelve, whether your car will touch thirty or sixty does not affect the principle — which should be an article of faith with every good motorist—viz.: that the car deserves all your assistance to develop the best service of which it is capable. Wherever or whatever you drive, modest little two - seater or stately limousine, you cannot provide your car with better help in its work than to equip it with

GOODRICH · TYRES

BEST IN THE LONG RUN

SAFETY FIRST

The Goodrich Safety Tread Tyre

The safety principle of this tyre is derived from the repetition of a moulded design of seven bars and a cross-tie moulded into the tread and forming a natural part of the tyre. Nothing could be simpler than the design or more efficient than its work. The seven longitudinal bars take a strong lateral grip of the road, the cross-ties clean and prepare the surface for the grip. Whatever the angle of the wheels, the formation of this tread offers the greatest possible resistance to side-slip. The tyre tends to transmit safety by forming a safety track. The rubber is incomparably tough and resilient. No tyre will travel rough surfaces with greater impunity or give a longer life.

GOODRICH
" FULL-SIZES "
CARRY THE LOAD

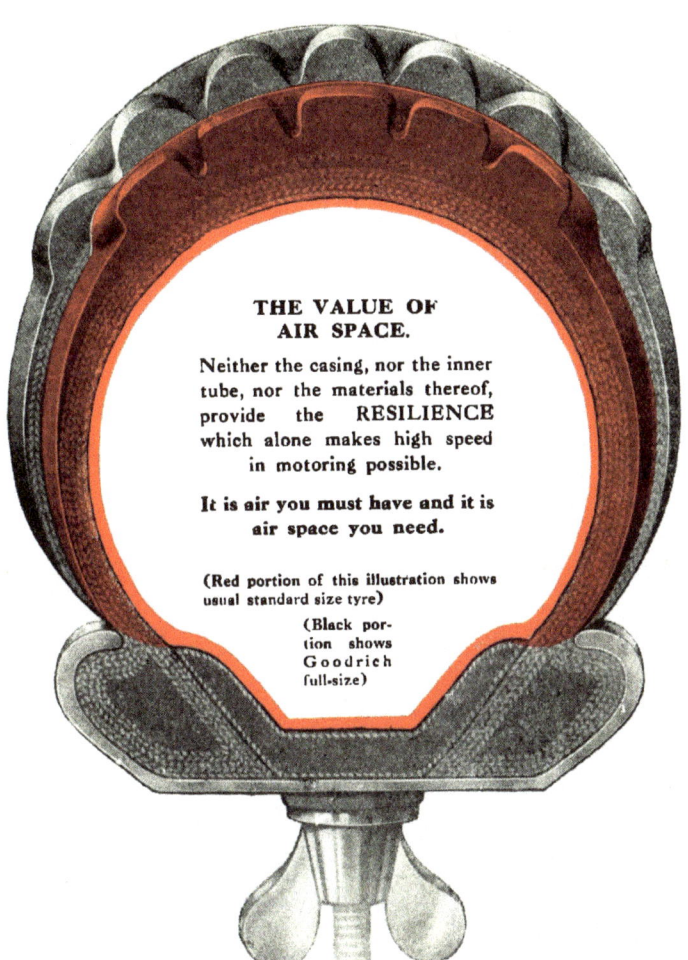

THE VALUE OF AIR SPACE.

Neither the casing, nor the inner tube, nor the materials thereof, provide the RESILIENCE which alone makes high speed in motoring possible.

It is air you must have and it is air space you need.

(Red portion of this illustration shows usual standard size tyre)

(Black portion shows Goodrich full-size)

GOODRICH FULL-SIZES
measure up to the specifications marked on them.

OVERLOADING is the cause of practically 75% of Pneumatic Tyre troubles, and overloading is simply another word for UNDERSIZING.

Under-sized tyres are expensive and destructive in every way—*and yet the standard range of European Millimètre FABRIC tyres, except Goodrich, measure less than their claimed dimensions, that is to say they are undersized.*

17

B

GOODRICH

the master
of the road

GOODRICH
Red
Inner Tubes

The Tube is the pivot upon which the whole pleasure and convenience of motoring turns. The Goodrich Company recognise this, and treat the Tube accordingly.

INNER TUBE CONSTRUCTION
reaches its highest point of efficiency
in the GOODRICH RED TUBE

EVERY TUBE REPRESENTS PERFECTION

ECONOMY

Economy, once a partially negligible virtue, has now become a daily necessity as well as a public duty. The modest residue left by the Chancellor must be carefully conserved and studiously expended.

An extra 500 or 1000 miles may not seem much, but it represents a percentage of profit you would like to see on every share you own or purchase you make.

To the motorist who uses his tyres as he would his horse, that is to say with consideration, who records mileages, tests values, and judges results, this extra margin is always to be obtained—*plus safety*, in

GOODRICH TYRES

:: *The Tyre of Super Service* ::

BEST IN THE LONG RUN

HOW TO TREAT YOUR TYRES

Why have not all tyres the same mileage ?

The reason lies, not as is usually supposed, in an irregularity of manufacture, and still less in the case of Goodrich whose quality of manufacture is maintained at a remarkably consistent level throughout ; it comes only from difference in treatment.

Someone has said : " **Man does not die, he only kills himself.**" This is true, and though it may seem exaggerated when applied to a tyre, it is not so. **More Tyres are killed by abuse than die from natural causes.**

It is acknowledged that the **GOODRICH** is the best tyre. Owing to its scientific manu-facture its quality is the best that has yet been produced, and it is maintained at an extremely high level.

It is no less true that it must be treated carefully —it is the least you owe to it—in exchange for the hard work you demand.

THE TWO CHIEF ENEMIES
of the TYRE are :

OVER INFLATION and
UNDER INFLATION

A normal load may be excessive if the inflation is not sufficient and inversely a normal inflation may not be sufficient if the load is excessive.

TYRE INFLATION

Tyre inflation tables are often misleading, since all pressures must be governed by the weight of the car. It is difficult to lay down a hard and fast rule on this point, especially when it is remembered that a 90 m/m tyre, for example, is often scheduled as standard specification for cars which vary in weight as much as 5 cwts. A sound rule is to inflate your tyres until they stand well up under the full load. Then test with a pressure gauge and make a note for future reference. Average pressures are—

65 m/m or 2½"	85 m/m or 3"	90 m/m or 3½"	100 m/m or 3½"	105 m/m or 4"	120 m/m or 4½"	135 m/m or 5"
45-50 lbs.	50-55 lbs.	55-60 lbs.	55-60 lbs.	60-65 lbs.	65-70 lbs.	70-75 lbs·

The 5 lb. variation indicated above is to provide for the difference between a light and full load, this being estimated at about 2 cwt.

The following precautions will also be found useful:

Check the alignment of the wheels.

Imperfect alignment puts an unlimited tax on your tyres and pocket.

Attend to cuts in the outer cover of tyres.

Don't neglect a cut. Small injuries often result in large bursts. Seal the cut and save the tyre.

Avoid non-skid chains

or other such non-skid devices fixed on the tyres.

The best and the least expensive means to avoid skidding is to use the GOODRICH SAFETY TREAD.

Avoid wheel tracks,

the car lines, etc., which cut your tyres on the sides.

Avoid contact with kerbs

when you reverse, the tyre suffers a violent shock often sufficient to tear the inner lining and cause a burst later on which will seem inexplicable.

Avoid bad repairs

which, under the pretext of being quick or cheap, never mend your tyres properly, but on the contrary expose you to great inconvenience and even accidents.

GOODRICH
SOLID BAND
TYRES

"The Defeat of Hercules"
Reproduced from the Goodrich
"Solid Tyres" Booklet.

The GOODRICH Company make not
only Pneumatic motor tyres but also
solid tyres for commercial vehicles.
This solid tyre differs from others by
its special construction which gives it a
much greater resistance and a longer life.

Special Features

of

GOODRICH Band Tyres

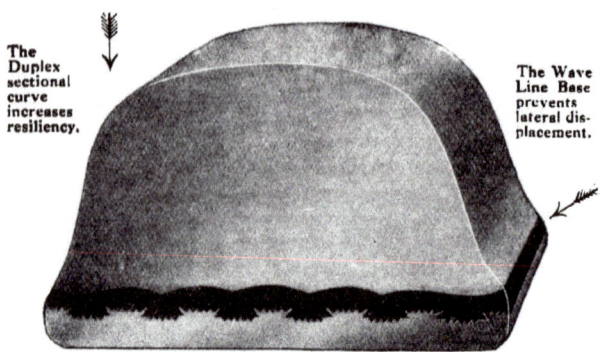

The Duplex sectional curve increases resiliency.

The Wave Line Base prevents lateral displacement.

The Wave Line Base. Instead of a flat upper surface upon the hard rubber sub-base which offers little resistance to lateral movement of the soft rubber under load, we developed the wave line, which not only prevents this displacement sideways, but greatly strengthens the union between the hard and soft rubber.

The Duplex Curve. Another improvement is in the shape of the tread. In place of the ordinary round profile, **GOODRICH Band Tyre** treads have a duplex curve, which makes them more resilient and durable than any other.

Specimen of Goodrich Road Sign.

Read the GOODRICH signs as you go along—they may save you much time and trouble.

VILLE

PNEU

GOODRICH

Nom des Agents dans cette ville

A specimen of the numerous Goodrich enamelled iron plates which the tourist will meet on the French roads.

OUR isolated road boards and our enamelled plates at the entrance of towns, supply the tourist with quick and precise information of the addresses where he can find not only

GOODRICH TYRES

but also petrol, oil, accessories, &c.

The value of all Goodrich publicity is that it is TRUE.

We do not say that our pneumatics and "solids" are everlasting,

we only say that
in the long run
they are the most economical.

Two Goodrich Posters.

The quality of GOODRICH products is un-
deniable, and for that reason we welcome
the only aid which advertising can give any
manufacturer, viz., to make known the good
qualities which are *inherent* in an article.
Advertising cannot confer quality upon an
article, it can only give distinction of presentation.

Visit to the War Regions

General Section Map and Alphabetical Index

ORDER OF EACH SECTOR.

Map—Route—Hotels—Historical and Economic Accounts—
Short Account of the Operations—War Facts.

THE WAR

FROM THE SEA TO THE VOSGES

The views of the monuments taken before the War and reproduced in this guide book will give some idea of the significance of the present destroyed aspect.

Since 1870 the world assisted at the tremendous development of the German Empire, of its industry and trade, of its army and navy. It was evident, and the Germans themselves proclaimed it loudly, that " Germania " planned to capture the world's supremacy. Consequently a war was inevitable in order to definitely settle and prescribe her will to the whole of Europe. The first pretext which presented itself as an excuse for an armed struggle was a good one. On June 28, 1914, the Archduke, heir to the throne of Austria, was murdered at Serajevo by a Serbian student. The government of Francis Joseph declares Serbia responsible for this crime, and on July 22, sends an ultimatum to the King of Serbia. This ultimatum is practically a declaration of war, since the enforcement of its conditions means the downfall of this small state's independence. The Serbians attempt to arrange matters in a way compatible with their national honour, but the Austrians are not satisfied. The Russians come to the defence of the Serbians, and mobilise. Moreover, Francis Joseph has already mobilised eight army corps, recalled his ambassador from Belgrade and proclaimed martial law.

On July 27, the French, British and Russian diplomats approach the Kaiser in order to obtain, through his influence on Austria, a conference to discuss the problems, but he refuses his help. On July 28, Austria declares war against Serbia. Events now proceed rapidly. At midday on August 1, the German mobilisation order is issued, and at four o'clock general mobilisation is ordered in France.

On August 2, the Germans declare war on Russia, invade the Grand Duchy of Luxemburg, break into French territory, and shoot a French soldier, although war has not yet been declared. On August 3, M. de Schoen, in the name of the German Empire, proclaims Germany at war with France.

The War

On August 4, England declares war on Germany and Austria, and the same day Italy announces that she will preserve her neutrality. This was a day of great surprises for Germany.

War has begun. Contrary to all the rights of nations, and in betrayal of their own word, the Germans enter Belgium, which has rejected their ultimatum. The treaty of 1831 is for these new Vandals only " a scrap of paper."

The gallant resistance of Liège was big with consequences for the Germans, for it prevented them taking the French army by surprise as they had intended. Out of revenge they put Belgium to fire and sword.

The French troops had been massed on the Lorraine front, but, in order to face any German attack, it was necessary to execute numerous movements of troops, from which resulted a great inferiority in man-power on our side at the shock battle of Charleroi, besides which there had been mistakes in the transmission of orders ; the result was our defeat and the necessity for retreat. This latter, called the Retreat of Charleroi, had its effect on the movements of those troops which had been already progressing into the annexed Alsace and Lorraine, and which necessarily had to withdraw also. It had, in addition, a serious influence on the movements of the British Expeditionary Force, under Sir John French, which had just previously checked the Germans with heavy loss at the battle of Mons. The British Commander was undoubtedly taken a great deal by surprise by this unsuspected man-œuvre, and the retreat which followed, precipitately undertaken under the pressure of extraneous events, was coloured with many unfortunate incidents, all indirectly due to the absence of proper liaison between the Allied armies. At this time only four British Divisions (or 100,000 men) had landed on French soil.

Compelled by force of circumstances to let the enemy penetrate French territory, General Joffre decided to retire until, reorganised and supported on a solid defensive basis, the army could turn against the enemy, resist him, and, taking the offensive, throw him back from Paris. This plan was executed in all its details, and the strategic retreat of Charleroi ended with the splendid victory of the Marne. The enemy was thus obliged to abandon his vainglorious hope of a swift entry into Paris. He went to earth in the rocks of Soissons, and from that moment began the laborious trench war which was to persist throughout the winter of 1914-15.

The British army, whose task it now became to prolong the Allied line north-eastwards, co-operated in all these movements ; and although during the retreat to the Marne some of its units became temporarily scattered, it reached that line unbroken in its formation, having successfully beaten off the enemy in three consecutive rear-guard actions.

31

The War

During the succeeding months of October and November the Germans attempted to establish their positions in the north. The British and French armies, jointly with the valiant Belgian troops, followed them in that race to the sea. Thrown back on the borders of Belgium, the Germans tried to break through our thinly held front and reach Calais, which resulted in the first battle of Ypres.

The Battle of Yser, as it is known in France, is universally recognised as our " First Battle of Ypres," one of the greatest and most heroic conflicts in which British troops have ever engaged. The efforts which the Germans exerted to break through our line and capture Calais were supported with such weight of artillery and men as had not previously been equalled. By the end of November the Germans had accumulated in this salient at least 750,000 troops, to oppose which the total Allied forces in the sector were not much more than 200,000. The supreme German attempt, which nearly succeeded, was made under the eyes of the Kaiser on October 29. Although some success was at first achieved, the vigour and resolution of the British resistance turned the issue, and by nightfall our position was once more secure. The loss was heavy on each side, but the ravages made in the German ranks who had advanced in mass formation, were terrible. The glorious termination of this battle is now commemorated as one of the most magnificent exploits of British arms.

In the mud our troops resisted the heavy shocks of the German army, and at the end of November the Allied armies could register a new victory when the Kaiser finally gave up the idea of taking Calais.

The winter of 1914–1915 was particularly terrible for our soldiers, as the trenches had not yet been organised as they were later. On May 9, 1915, the French army attacked in the Artois, the objective being the plain of Lens. After the first successes, we were compelled to give up for the moment the idea of breaking through. A second attempt, carried out in September in the Champagne and Artois sectors, gave the same result : we made numerous prisoners, we progressed steadily at the commencement, but no strategic results were obtained.

In September 1915 an English offensive in the region of Loos and Hulluch was launched ; the first-line objectives were gained, and, in some places, passed, but only in the face of sustained artillery fire and at the cost of heavy losses. It was eventually decided not to pursue the attack further. At the end of the year Sir Douglas Haig succeeded Sir John French in supreme command of the British Forces.

At the commencement of 1916 the Germans inaugurated a " colossal " offensive against Verdun. The attack was launched on February 21. At first it seemed that the old fortress would have to give way before the enormous masses of men, which, preceded by terrific bombardments, were hurled without ceasing against the outlying posts. She held out, thanks to the splendid heroism, and after one year and a half of frightful carnage the enemy were forced to give up the attempt, not, however, without having suffered tremendous losses. Verdun is, with the Marne, the most glorious of all French victories.

The constant German pressure on Verdun, which had reached its culminating point in June 1916, necessitated the preparation of a direct Allied counter-effort on some other sector of the Western Front. For this purpose, General Haig placed both himself and his armies at the immediate disposal of the French High Command ; and, after a week of sustained activity by the artillery, a great offensive was launched on a huge front in the region of the Somme on July 1. The attack was completely successful, and is especially noteworthy as being the occasion on which that British invention, "The Tank," was first used in overcoming the almost insuperable defensive possibilities of perfected trench warfare. Though the weather conditions at that period were most unsuitable, our troops continued their unwavering advance for three months with hardly a check, and finally forced the enemy in desperation to adopt a policy of wholesale and ruthless destruction of roads, woods and property in the hope, unfortunately justified by results, of preventing a really vital enlargement of our gains. The fighting during this battle was carried on with a degree of violence and reckless courage on both sides amazing to witness, but in the face of trench systems organised for defence in the most modern manner, our relentless advance reflected great credit on the new army.

From July, 1916, the French Army, in concert with the British, took the offensive and gained fine successes in the Somme sector. Our progress in this region forced the Germans in March, 1917, to abandon positions which they had kept since 1914, and to retire on the banks of the Oise. This was known as the retreat of St. Quentin.

Unfortunately, this retreat disorganised our plans, with the result that the offensive of 1917 could not produce the desired effect of surprise. On April 16, French troops, attacking in the sectors of the Chemin des Dames and Moronvilliers with the hope of breaking through, succeeded only in winning local successes ; the German front flinched slightly. Other local successes ; at Verdun, at the Malmaison, in the British sector of Cambrai, and in Flanders, complete our balance for 1917. Meanwhile, the Russian Revolution having turned into anarchy, the Germans were able to dispose freely of the greatest part of their forces in Russia, and make up enormous bodies of reserves which, at an appointed day, would become the nucleus of a tremendous offensive.

The only success of any great importance secured by the British in the year 1917, was the capture of the dominating chain of small hills known as the Messines-Wytschaete Ridge on June 7, 1917. This feat, remarkable on account of the unparalleled strength of the defence works, was only accomplished by the creation of two huge underground mining galleries, planned on a stupendous scale and containing over a million pounds of explosive, which were blown up with great effect on the morning of the attack. In addition to these two monsters, 17 other mines were exploded on the front simultaneously and their concerted effect on the morale and organisation of the enemy was incalculable. To some extent their power may be judged by the following results, for the whole of the strongly entrenched Messines Ridge was taken in twenty-four hours. An advance of such rapidity may well be attributed almost wholly to the influence of these terrible engines.

A further offensive in the Ypres region was carried out on July 31 of this year, with the intention of definitely delivering the Ypres salient from all future operations of the Germans. The progress of the offensive was necessarily much more deliberate, by reason of the nature of the ground and the wide area involved. Indeed, the final " push " was not brought to its inevitable conclusion before the end of October, but such was the magnitude of the task undertaken that only those personally concerned could realise its difficulties. The weather conditions, always vital to the success of an operation, were at their very worst, the resistance was obstinate and bitter, and the difficulties of transport and supply were so arduous as to make them frequently appear impossible of solution. In the face of all these factors our men pursued their aim unflinchingly, and by their unshakable courage and determination accomplished a performance which will for ever shed a glorious lustre on the valour of our arms.

On May 27, after two months of relative inaction, the Germans took us by surprise at the Chemin-des-Dames, and hustling our weak military posts, succeeded in progressing rapidly as far as Chateau-Thierry. Paris was again threatened. Once again our troops broke the shock of the enemy, who was forced to stop on the skirts of the woods of Villers-Cotterets, unable to cross the Marne. In spite of the serious losses it had suffered, the power of the German army was not yet broken. It attempted a supreme effort on July 15 in the Champagne, and failed before the ability of General Gouraud. Three days later, on July 18, General Mangin counter-attacked, and after 15 days he cleared "the pocket" of Chateau-Thierry. In the words of General Foch, " we began to descend the slope again."

From this time we have to record only magnificent victories. Debeney's army attacking in Picardy on August 8, takes Montdidier and progresses splendidly. In September the Americans take Saint Mihiel in one bound, the Belgians and British progress in Flanders. Gouraud attacks in Champagne. The enemy is everywhere retreating. The deliverance of Belgium has begun ; there is left only one strip of land when, on November 11, under the menace of a big offensive in Lorraine, the enemy asks for mercy, and signs the armistice. It was Victory ; our troops entering Lorraine and Alsace were the centre of indescribable enthusiasm, and then they occupied the Prussian Rhineland.

On June 28, 1919, Peace was signed at Versailles. Right triumphed over Force. France had conquered her hereditary enemy, thanks

The War

to the bravery of her sons, to the bravery of her Allies, and to the young American army which had landed on the old Gallic soil at the critical hour when the Germans were about to shout as in 1914, " Nach Paris."

We have been unable to conduct the tourist to every spot of the battle line which merits attention. We have cited only those places which, frequently met with in the Communiques of the Allied armies, will remain famous in the history of the war because they were either the seats of decisive battles or of sanguinary combats. But every village and valley, every ridge and field, and every wood where our soldiers have fought, where they have shed their blood and sacrificed their lives for the defence of right and liberty, are holy places, to be visited only with the saintly devotion of a pilgrimage. There is no point on the immense battle-line from Switzerland to the North Sea which has not been the witness of the courage, spirit of sacrifice, of the devotion and heroism, which for fifty-two months have animated the hearts of millions of men. From the battlefield of the Marne to the valleys of Morhange, from Altkirch to Funnes, the tourist will see everywhere small wooden crosses marking the spots where underneath their earth mantles sleep such heroes as history has never known. He will recognise the graves of French soldiers by the tri-colour cockades adorning them ; alas ! they are also the most numerous. Contemplating these, whatever may be the nationality of the tourist, he will be unable to refrain from a feeling of profound admiration for the people who, with such splendid enthusiasm, raised themselves against the barbarous invader ; making of the breasts of all her sons a living rampart to the old Latin civilisation, its liberties and rights.

On September 6, 1914, France saved the world from barbarism. She made a firm stand for more than four years against an enemy marshalled for her ruin. With her Allies' help, she has conquered. Glory to all those who have died for her and now sleep in their old French soil.

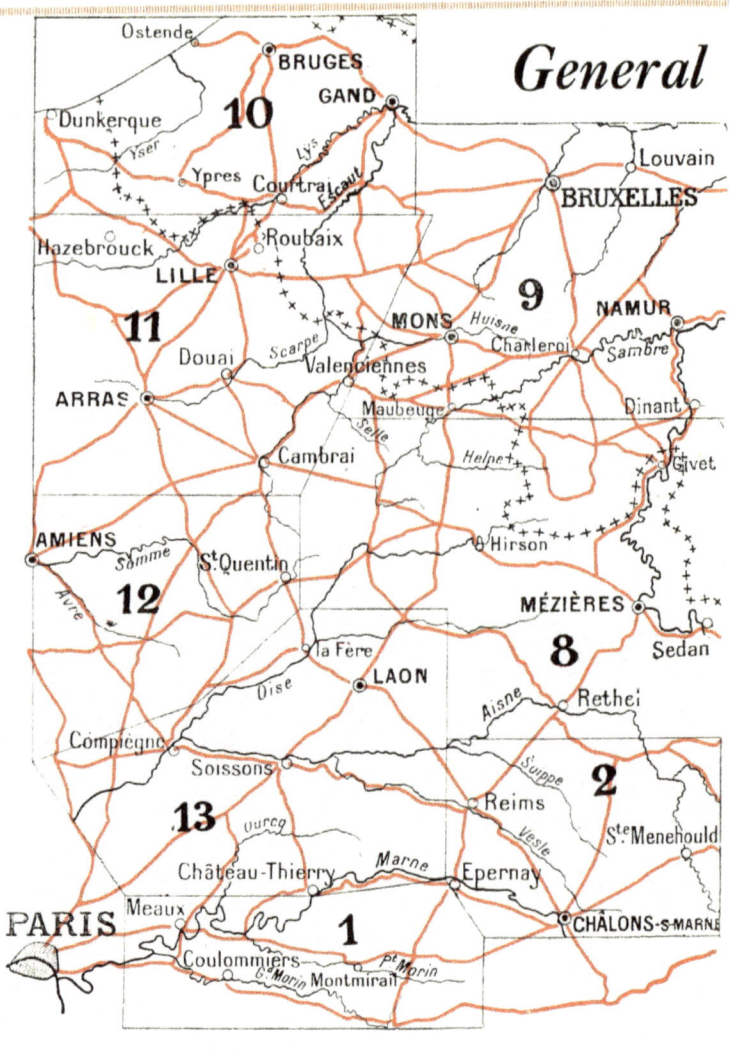

General

Metz	409 Kil.	Ostende	345 Kil.
Mézières	245 „	Pont-à-Mousson	381 „
Mons..........	305 „	Reims	156 „
Montmédy	298 „	Rethel	248 „
Montmirail	72 „	Roubaix	262 „
Mulhouse	485 „	Saint-Dié	433 „
Namur	377 „	Saint-Quentin .	146 „
Nancy	353 „	Ste.-Menehould	215 „

Map of the Sectors

Distance from Paris to the Principal Towns

Amiens	131 Kil.	Douai	218 Kil.
Arras	192 ,,	Dunkerque	305 ,,
Bar-le-Duc	254 ,,	Epernay	125 ,,
Belfort	443 ,,	La Fère	138 ,,
Briey	331 ,,	Gand	340 ,,
Bruges	365 ,,	Givet	305 ,,
Bruxelles	310 ,,	Hazevrouck	302 ,,
Cambrai	178 ,,	Hirson	190 ,,
Chalons-S.-		Laon	140 ,,
Marne	173 ,,	Liège	455 ,,
Charleroi	337 ,,	Lille	250 ,,
Chateau-Thierry	98 ,,	Longwy	368 ,,
Colmar	473 ,,	Louvain	340 ,,
Compiègne	84 ,,	Lunéville	383 ,,
Coulommiers	60 ,,	Maubeuge	292 ,,
Courtrai	280 ,,	Meaux	38 ,,
Dinant	387 ,,		

Saint-Mihiel	315 Kil.
Saverne	470 ,,
Sedan	265 ,,
Soissons	108 ,,
Strasbourg	503 ,,
Toul	328 ,,
Valenciennes	256 ,,
Verdun	304 ,,
Ypres	294 ,,

Alphabetical List
and Famous

of Towns, Sites, Positions

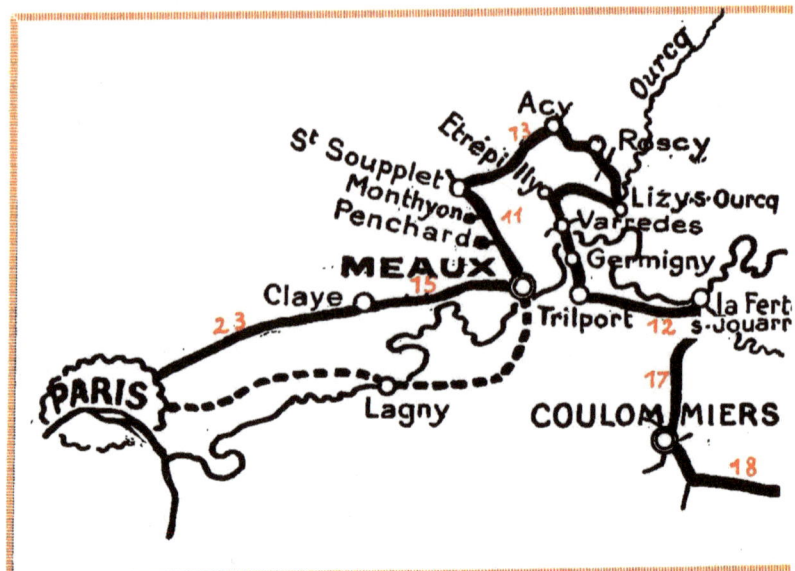

Sector 1—The Marne

Route

From *Paris* reach *Meaux* through *Claye* or *Lagny*. After visiting Meaux the tourist will take the roads of *Saint-Soupplet* and afterwards *Penchard* and *Monthyon*, the battlefields of Maunoury's army. At Saint-Soupplet, turn to the right, go to *Acy* and to *Roscu-en-Multien*, gain the borders of the Ourcq at *Lizy-sur-Ourcq*, there turn to the right and visit at *Etrepilly* the splendid monument raised to the dead of the Marne Battle, then retrace his route through *Varreddes*, *Germigny* and *Trilport*. From Trilport follow the Marne to *La Fert'-sous-Jouarre*, then come down to *Coulommiers*.

From Coulommiers reach *Esternay* by *Fert'-Gaucher*. The tourist will start with the battlefield of General Foch's army. From Esternay he will proceed to *Montmirail*, and thence to *Champaubert*.

From Champaubert, through *Baye*, proceed to *Sézanne*.

From Sézanne follow the railroad up to *Connantre* (an important supply station during the war) and *Fere-Champenoise*. Observe the numerous tombs on the railroad slope. From Fère Champenoise proceed to *Goizard*, situated amongst *Saint-Gond's* marshes, then from Goizard reach *Bergeres*, *Avize* and *Epernay*.

40

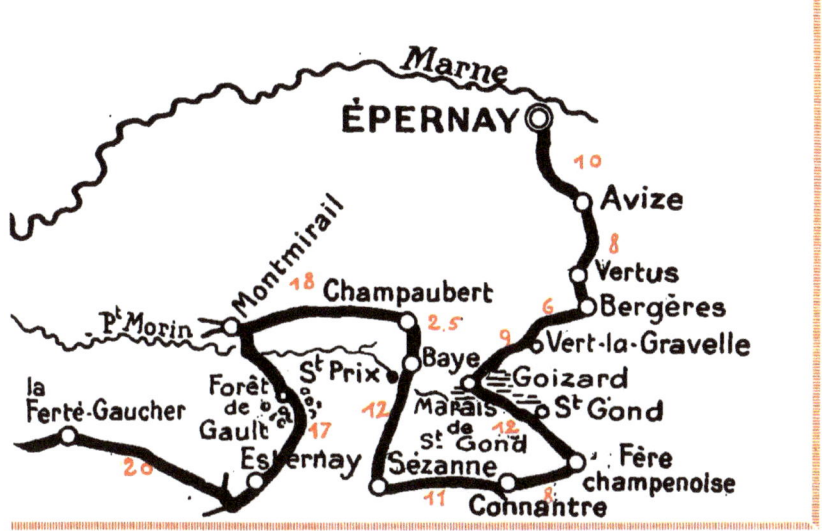

HOTELS

CHANTILLY
    HÔTEL D'ANGLETERRE.   Modern comfort.
      Place de l'Hospice.   Auto Garage.
      Owner: LESAGE-CHOCART.   Telephone 59.

COULOMMIERS
    HÔTEL DU SOLEIL-LEVANT.,   T.C.F.—A.C.F.
    Rue de Melun.
    Telephone 22.
    Owner: VEUVE ALBERT POIRE.

CRIEL
    HÔTEL DU CHEMIN DE FER.   Modern comfort.
    Avenue de la Gare.   Recommended by the T.C.F.
    Telephone 5.   Diploma. Garage with pit.

ÉPERNAY
    GRAND HÔTEL DE L'EUROPE. 30 comfortable rooms.
    Rue Porte Lucas.   Electric Lighting.   Garage.
    HOTEL MODERNE.   Central Heating.   Electric
    6 rue des Berceaux.   Lighting. Comfort. Garage.

FÈRE CHAMPENOISE
    HÔTEL DE PARIS.   Good kitchen.
    Rue de Maréchal Joffre.
    Owner: CHARLES LARCHET.
    Telephone 6.

MEAUX
HÔTEL DE LA SIRENE.   30 rooms.   Electric Lighting.
34 Rue Saint-Nicolas.   Modern comfort.

MONTMIRAIL
HÔTEL DE LA TOUR D'AUVERGNE.
Owner : LESCOURTIER-FOLLEAS.   Rooms T.C.F.
Auto-garage.

SENLIS
HÔTEL DE GRAND CERF.   All modern comfort.
Rue de la République.   American bar.   Garage.
(Rue Nationale 17).

SÉZANNE
HÔTEL DE FRANCE.   Modern comfort.
Grande Rue.   Very famous Cusine.
Owner : LOZE.   Garage.

Historical Account

The region where the Battle of the Marne was unrolled had already known invasion twice during the course of the nineteenth century. In 1814 the Allies (British, Prussians, Austrians and Russians) pursued there the army of the conquered Napoleon. The Emperor showed, in that retreat, the highest military qualities. With his so-called "Marie-Louise" he fought the glorious battles of Champaubert, Montmirail, Chateau-Thierry and Vauchamps ; in 1870 this region was occupied by the enemy after the defeat of the Châlons army at Sedan. It was evacuated after the surrender of Paris and the armistice of Versailles.

Economical Account

The largest part of Marne's battlefield is made up by the region commonly called "La Brie." It is an exclusively agricultural district of large estates, where the production of corn and sugar-beet is practised according to the most modern methods. The beet pulp is used for the breeding of famous oxen.

There is no other industry except the sugar manufacture, but, on the other hand, the numerous quarries have provided, and are providing still, the dressed ashlar, the chalk and plaster necessary for the construction and enlargement of Paris.

The marshes of Saint-Gond are unexploited turf-pits, out of which large quantities of a fuel not to be disdained could be easily be extracted. The western part of the battlefield is included in Champagne, and is made up of hills known under the name of the "cliffs of the island of France" ; these calcareous, dry, but fertile and well-exposed hills bear the fine vineyards, producing the famous champagne wines. Epernay is noted for underground cellars where the bottles of champagne are piled up by hundreds of thousands. One of these cellars reaches an area of 15 kilometres.

Ph. Rol

Gen. GALLIENY

Ph. Meley

Marshal JOFFRE

Ph. Rol

Gen. MAUNOURY

Short Account of the Operations

The Battle of the Marne remains the most magnificent work of the French army : there, our soldiers saved the world. It was the decisive battle, and had we lost it our Latin civilisation would have been ended, right would have yielded to brute force. This victory is due to the courage and heroism of the troops, but far more to the science and energy of the commanders. It was a skilful manœuvre which allowed us to conquer, and it may be mentioned that the Marne is the unique battle of this war in which *manœuvre alone* gave us victory. We were, indeed, quite out-numbered by the Germans, in men as well as in guns ; we had no heavy artillery, whereas the Germans had from the very beginning of the war numerous field howitzers ; nevertheless, we conquered on a front of 180 kilometres.

After the failure at Charleroi of our Belgian offensive, General Joffre had to give the general order of retreat as from August 25, 1914. His opinion was that the French army ought to retire until it was able to reorganise itself on more solid positions, thanks to such reinforcements that would enable it to arrest the enemy and throw him back on his borders. The plan of this retreat was scrupulously carried out, and the French army extended in half a circle before Paris like an immense net.

Ph. Rol

Marshal FRENCH

Ph. Meley

Marshal FOCH

Ph. Rol

Gen. FRANCHE D'ESPEREY

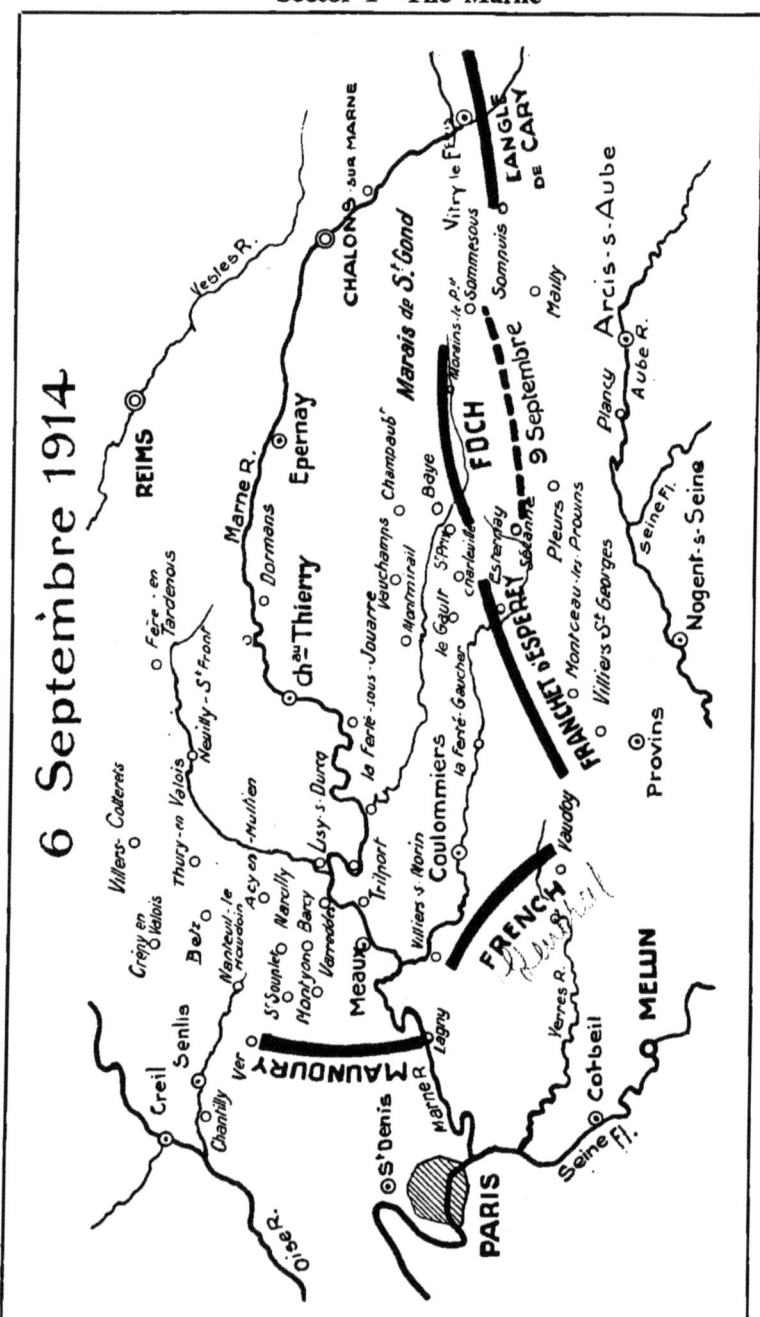

6 Septembre 1914

BATTLEFIELD OF THE MARNE

Sector 1—The Marne

The forces under the command of Sir John French occupied the extreme left of the allied lines, and were mainly occupied during the course of the retreat and in the subsequent advance in preventing the enemy from engaging in any turning movement on the coast.

On September 5 the various armies were occupying the position shown on the map, page 44. Maunoury's army on our left stretched out from Nanteuil-le-Haudouin to Lagny. The army of General French was prolonged to the south of Coulommiers from Hautefeuilles to Vaudoy ; on his right from Vaudoy to Sézanne, Franchet-d'Espérey's army was in position. To the east, Foch's army stretched out on a front going from Sézanne to Mailly's camp.

Joffre was determined to face the enemy. Von Kluck, who commands the invading army, begins to realise our will to resist. On September 5, Joffre issued from Claye this stirring order to his troops :

" At this moment, when a battle upon which depends the salvation of the country is about to begin, all our efforts must be concentrated on attacking and driving back the enemy. Under these circumstances no sign of weakness will be tolerated. The hour has come when we must stand fast whatever the cost, and accept death rather than give way. . . ."

From his side the German General Von Kluck addressed his soldiers as follows :

" To-morrow Germany's armies as well as our own army corps will be engaged on the whole line between Paris and Verdun in order to save the welfare and honour of our country. I expect each officer and soldier to do his duty fully and to the last breath in spite of the hard and heroic fights of these last days.

" Everything will depend on to-morrow's results . . ."

Our advance began on September 5, in the afternoon. Maunoury was trying to outflank Von Kluck's right wing, whilst Franchet-d'Espérey, on September 6, was making a serious advance. Von Kluck, realising the danger, threw himself desperately on Maunoury's army, which sustained the shock firmly. Meanwhile, the British Army and Franchet-d'Espérey continually advanced. Eventually Von Kluck was forced to retire and relinquish his hold on the rivers of the Ourcq. Checked before Paris, General Moltke launched General Von Hausen's army against that of Foch, assigning to them the mission of breaking through the French front.

The Germans threw themselves furiously on our centre, but happily they encountered a commander and troops such as were above all praise. Following an initial advance they suffered several bloody reverses, and finally they had to retire. A part of Von Hausen's army ran into Saint-Gond's marshes, and were decimated by the fire of our 75's. On the 12th, the enemy, having crossed the Aisne and settled down in the trenches prepared by his engineers during the retreat, began the long and awful war to gain the advantageous positions.

One of the decisive actions of this battle was the intervention of the 20,000 men sent in taxi-cabs by General Gallieni (at that time Governor of Paris) in order to rescue Maunoury's army.

This unexpected reinforcement enabled our left wing to withstand the awful shock of Von Kluck's troops. Another important move was the infiltration between Von Kluck's and Von Hausen's armies of a whole body of cavalry, upsetting the liaisons and bringing confusion into the German army.

The consequences of this battle were tremendous. The enemy retired 80 kilometres. More than a million Germans had rushed on Paris with 4,000 field guns and 450 heavy batteries. After several days' fighting they left on the ground 25,000 prisoners, 160 guns and a vast quantity of ammunition.

Above all they lost their immense hope of victory. General Von Moltke had the courage to confess to the Kaiser that " the war had been lost," an expression of opinion for which he was afterwards disgraced.

War Facts

CLAYE.—From Claye Joffre launched the famous order of September 5th. The villa which G.H.Q. occupied at the time of the Marne battle is at the entrance of Claye on the left side of the road to Paris when coming from Mitry.

LAGNY.—Here the bridge was blown up by the French engineers.

MEAUX.—A small town of about 14,000 inhabitants. Very curious cathedral of a Gothic style, having in the interior the monument of Bossuet and a pulpit made of the same panels as the one in which the famous speaker had preached.

Meaux has seen only a few groups of German scouts. A few shells burst in the neighbourhood of the cathedral and in the outskirts of St. Nicolas, but caused little damage. The British retreating troops blew up the bridges.

PENCHARD.—Here was the opening of the Marne Battle; the Morocco brigade on September 5, at 2 p.m., attacked the village, and after an obstinate engagement succeeded in occupying it, but had to evacuate it shortly after; on the 6th they again attacked and this time Penchard was definitely abandoned by the enemy.

MONTHYON was attacked at the same time as Penchard, but the German machine guns broke the onset of our infantry. On the 6th, however, they had to give up the strong position of Monthyon, as they were threatened with a flanking movement.

FERME DE NOGEON.—Now rebuilt, was destroyed almost completely by the German shells. Here many engagements took place, and particularly at night; in the course of one of them a French soldier captured the colours of a German regiment after having stabbed the ensign with his bayonet.

ACY-EN-MULTIEN was taken and retaken several times at the price of heavy losses on both sides.

TROCY.—Numerous German batteries were stationed at Trocy,and a certain number of houses were destroyed by our own ·75 batteries.

ETREPILLY.—A superb monument has been erected on the site of the heaviest fighting for the conquest of the plateau. It was here that the 20,000 men sent in taxi-cabs by General Gallieni to the rescue of Maunoury's army were discharged. This was a precious and unexpected help which brought quite near the line of fire those small automobiles. It was the first utilisation of motor cars for the transportation of troops.

These taxi-cabs had to run between Paris and Etrepilly several times on roads already broken by the shells and the passage of numerous artillery and supply transports. Goodrich Tyres rendered magnificent service during this transport work.

VARREDDES.—When the Germans abandoned Varreddes they took with them twenty hostages chosen from amongst the old people. The first day they walked 30 kilometres ; seven of them fell down from exhaustion and were killed with rifle butts.

It was in the neighbourhood of Varreddes that, after 17 attempts, the British succeeded in establishing a pontoon bridge under heavy fire of machine guns and artillery.

TRILPORT.—At the moment when our troops were retreating, the French engineers blew up one arch of the Marne Bridge here. A little after that, a motor car in which were two Americans enlisted in the French army, was rushing at full speed at the bridge, and was precipitated into the Marne. The two passengers were safely rescued, but perished afterwards, victims of their courage in attempting to gather from the enemy useful information for their commanding officer.

COULOMMIERS was occupied for a few days by the Germans. Her aldermen and M. Bargy, the Public Prosecutor, behaved in the presence of the German soldiers with a dignity which is beyond every praise.

ESTERNAY was taken by an infantry division of Franchet-d'Espérey's army. This division, by slipping through the wood of La Noue, had succeeded in turning the enemy's defence works. 8,000 Germans lay on the field of battle after the engagement in Esternay and the neighbourhood. A German ambulance was installed in the church. Most of the houses had been methodically looted. Several civilians, among others, a young girl of twenty were killed by the German soldiers. At Champigny they martyred in a fearful way a poor man, Mr. Louvet, in the presence of his own wife.

FORET-LE-GAULT.—A whole German battalion was captured here and much important material seized : ammunition, machine guns and trucks.

MONTMIRAIL was the scene of many obstinate fights. The Germans clung to it desperately ; the contest was a violent one and lasted more than eight hours. In the evening we occupied the position on which 7,000 German corpses were found.

CHAMPAUBERT has remained famous since the battle which Napoleon delivered here in 1814, during the French campaign.

A commemorative column has been erected in front of the house where Napoleon slept.

Champaubert was reconquered by Foch's army on September 10, 1914.

BAYE.—The castle, in which Marion Delorme was born, was inhabited by some Prince of the German Imperial family, probably by the Duke of Brunswick, son-in-law of the Kaiser, who behaved like a bandit, causing desks, silver cabinets and safes to be opened to obtain the money and rich artistic collections they contained.

SAINT-PRIX was the scene of a terrible combat ; the colonial troops, nevertheless, got hold of this village in a few hours, in spite of the thousands of shells with which the German artillery decimated them.

CHATEAU-DE-MONDEMENT.—The Castle was taken at dawn on September 9 by the Germans, who immediately organised it for defence. But a brave regiment (the 77th Infantry) was ready to counter-attack. They attacked on one side of the castle while the Zouaves attacked on the other. At 14.20 p.m. the attack begins, but only one breach has been opened in the walls ; Major Beaufort and all those who succeed him fall under the storm of the German shells.

A few men, using their backs for a ladder, attempt to pass over the wall, but hardly one appears on the top when a bullet kills him. Not being strong enough to get hold of the castle, they have to retire slightly. In order to destroy the castle, they bring in their arms .75 guns and fix them at a distance of 900 to 1,200 feet. A fearful fire opens, the walls of the castle fall down under this direct bombardment, the defence becomes impossible for the Germans, and when our troops storm again in the evening they find the approaches of the castle covered with grey corpses.

FERE CHAMPENOISE.—On September 8, Fere Champenoise fell into the hands of the Germans during Von Hausen's offensive against Foch. On September 9 the reserve troops quartered in town were just about to celebrate gaily the victories of the Empire, the wine was flowing in the well-supplied cellars, the empty champagne bottles covered the streets, and the fantastic, big German soldiers, at the sound of the fifes, were dancing, masquerading in women's clothes stolen from a neighbouring house. But General Foch had already retaken the offensive and was progressing rapidly ; an order to retreat unexpectedly tore the Germans away from their orgies.

Meanwhile, heavy battles were being delivered on the large plain west of Fère. This plain is studded with small thickets of stunted pines, which constituted excellent positions of resistance for the retreating enemy. Hidden behind the trees, the Germans let our soldiers approach to a good shooting range and by a sudden volley they tried to kill as many men as possible and throw panic in our ranks. Fortunately, the 75's were all the time shelling these small thickets with devastating shrapnel, and brought a general confusion among the enemy's troops. On September 10 General Foch established his quarters at Fère Champenoise.

THE MARSHES OF SAINT-GOND.—Our troops had to leave the marshes on September 7, but Foch's army having resumed the offensive on the 10th, they succeeded rapidly in getting hold of the ridges which command them. Our 75's were established there, and their terrible fire cut to pieces the Prussian guards who were trying vainly to defend the marshes. 8,000 men belonging to the élite battalions found their death in the turf-pits of Saint-Gond.

They had not been caught in the marshes, as it has been said, their commanding officers having known perfectly well all the practicable paths, thanks to their intelligence service before the war. But, being located in this basin, and impeding each other on the roads and paths, they were unable to scatter in order to escape the fire of our guns ; and it was impossible, under these conditions, to dig themselves in.

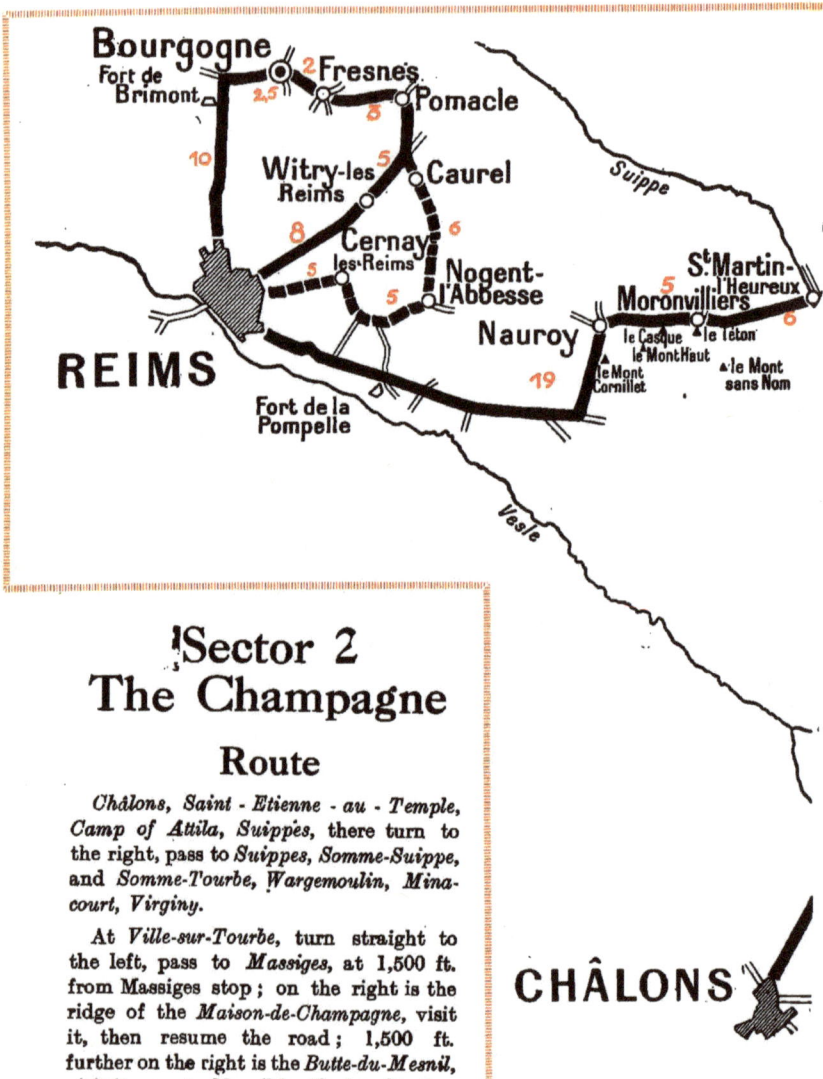

Sector 2
The Champagne

Route

Châlons, Saint - Etienne - au - Temple, Camp of Attila, Suippes, there turn to the right, pass to *Suippes, Somme-Suippe,* and *Somme-Tourbe, Wargemoulin, Mina-court, Virginy.*

At *Ville-sur-Tourbe,* turn straight to the left, pass to *Massiges,* at 1,500 ft. from Massiges stop ; on the right is the ridge of the *Maison-de-Champagne,* visit it, then resume the road ; 1,500 ft. further on the right is the *Butte-du-Mesnil,* visit it, pass to *Mesnil-les-Hurlus, Perthes-les-Hurlus.*

Now turn to the right, pass to Tahure, on the north is the famous *Butte-de-Tahure.* Follow the route of *Somme-Py* about 300 ft. and turn to the left towards *Souain.*

At Souain turn to the right and ascend towards *Somme-Py,* on the right you will see the *Butte-de-Souain* and the farm *Navarin,* at Somme-

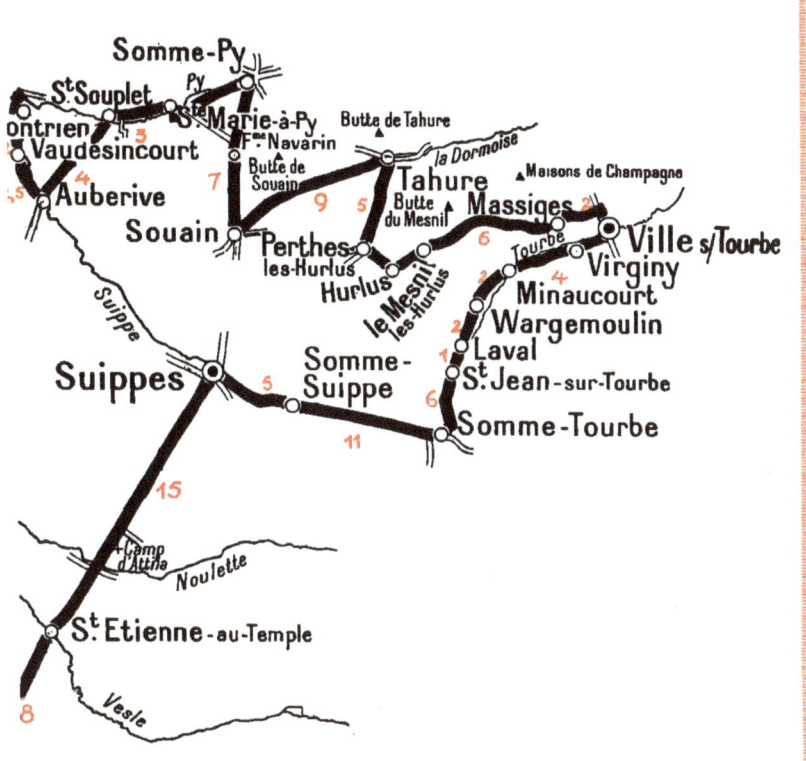

Py turn to the left for *Auberive*, there turn to the right, follow the *Suippe*, pass on to *Vaudesincourt*, *Dontrien*; at Dontrien turn to the left towards *Nauroy*. You will see first on the left the *Mont-Sans-Nom*, then the *Téton*, then the *Casque*, the *Mont Haut* and *Mont Cornillet*. At Nauroy, turn to the left, retake the main road of Suippes to *Reims*, follow it towards Reims, on the way you will note the *Fort de la Pompelle*.

Reims, *Fort de Brimont*, there turn to the right and come back by the main road, which you follow as far as *Nogent-l'Abbesse* and return through *Cernay-les-Reims*.

|||||||||||||||||||||||||||||||||||||||||||||||||||||||||||||||||||||||||||||||||||||||||||||||||||||||||

HOTELS

CHALONS-SUR-MARNE

HOTEL DU RENARD,
  Place de la République.

40 Rooms. Modern comfort.
Central heating. Garage.

GRAND HOTEL CENTRAL ET D'ANGLETERRE,
  1 rue de la Gravière.

Modern comfort. Garage.

REIMS

GRAND HOTEL DU NORD,
  Place Drouet d'Erlon.

50 rooms. Electric Lighting.
Garage.

GRAND HOTEL CONTINENTAL,
  Place Drouet d'Erlon.

Central heating. Garage.
Comfort.

ANNEXE DU GRAND HOTEL,
  50 Rue Clovis.

Comfortable rooms. Good
kitchen.

HOTEL DE CHAMPAGNE,
  Bld. de la République.

VITRY-LE-FRANÇOIS

GRAND HOTEL DE LA CLOCHE, Modern comfort. Garage.
  Rue de Frignicourt.
Centre of the town in front of the station.

Historical Account

Champagne is one of the oldest of French provinces ; in the Middle Ages it was particularly prosperous and the fairs of Reims and Châlons were famous. It had to suffer very much from the invasions of 1814 and 1817, and it has not been spared in 1914.

Reims is a very old town whose prosperity has always been on the increase. In her cathedral, which is a marvel of the French architectural art, the Kings of France were once crowned. It was there that Jeanne d'Arc caused her " gentle king " to be crowned. All those who have known Reims before the war cannot help cursing the Germans, who, without any military reason, have destroyed such masterpieces, like the cathedral, the church of Saint-Rémy, the archbishop's palace and the Town Hall, and turned this prosperous town into a heap of ruins.

Industrial Account

Besides the cliff of the Island of France, which has been referred to in the Sector 1, and which is the large vine region, Champagne comprises two quite distinct parts ; the damp, wooded, fertile Champagne, very suitable for breeding, and the wretched, dry and barren steppe where they practise only the herding of sheep. This latter has made Reims the home of a very prosperous wool trade. Châlons and Reims are, with Epernay, the centres of the Champagne wine trade.

Short Account of the Operations

Ph. Meley

Gen. GOURAUD

Ph. Meley

Gen. MARCHAND

The region comprised between Reims, Epernay, Sainte-Ménehould and Vouziers was the theatre of two great battles during this war, the French offensive on September 25, 1915, and the German offensive on July 15, 1918.

In these two offensives one meets again the characteristics of every battle since 1915, but with this difference ; in the first, our bombardment was of a long duration, and, our initial spring once arrested, we sought to progress slowly with trench warfare methods ; on the contrary, the German attack was preceded by an extremely violent but short bombardment, and when the impetus of the German masses was broken against the organisations of the second line, to which we had retired, the enemy did not attempt to progress by means of local engagements.

The offensive of September 25, 1915, was launched on the front Auberive-Ville-sur-Tourbe, after 4 days' violent bombardment.

We had no big shells, but for the first time the enemy suffered a continuous bombardment of a long duration, and opposed no resistance to our storm. We seized in the German trenches 25,000 prisoners and 150 guns after an offensive of 5 or 6 days. As we were lacking in long-range guns, our troops could not reach the organisation of the second line, which had not suffered from our fire.

On July 15, 1918, the Germans proceeded to carry out a gigantic offensive. They had massed on the eastern front of Verdun 170,000 men in the first line, and as many in reserve. They were hoping to advance as far as Châlons, and cut the French army in two. General Gouraud, who commanded our army in Champagne, was well informed of the enemy's preparations. The day before the attack he made a retirement of a few miles, abandoning those positions which it would have been impossible to hold under the enemy's bombardments. Five minutes before the Germans began their opening fire he ordered a counter preparation fire, which made tremendous devastation among the German regiments, massed there for the assault. The Germans stormed our first line but found there only a few blocks of machine guns, which, solidly built, had resisted the destructive fire and caused them many losses.

When they reached our second line, which had not been touched yet, they were greeted by the curtain fire of the 155's and the 75's with such violence that they suffered altogether 40,000 casualties, killed and wounded, during this one day, whereas Gouraud lost only 5,000 men. The Germans could not even entirely hold the narrow strips of land which we had freely abandoned to them.

From Mont-Blanc William II and Ludendorff assisted at the failure of the supreme effort of their armies.

Besides these two battles, properly called the " Battles of Champagne," we must mention the French attack of April 1916, in the region of the Monts. A few notes will be found on this attack, page 55, Article : Moronvilliers.

The Germans finally abandoned the left sector of their Champagne positions on October 5, 1918, and the right on the 11th. The Crown Prince had to withdraw his troops to Vouziers, then to Rethel ; only the armistice put an end to his disasters.

War Items

MASSIGES.—The Massiges Ridge, like an enormous flank bastion, secured the defence of a great part of the German front in the Champagne, stretching into five small crests shaped like the five fingers of the hand, and was therefore named the " Main de Massiges " (hand of Massiges). The Germans believed this sector to be invulnerable. " With two orderlies and one machine gun we could hold Massiges," they said.

On September 25 the approaches to this position were brilliantly conquered by the Moroccan troops. From September 25 to the 30th the colonials were progressing methodically along the fingers of the hand, and on the 30th the central bastion was taken.

The German trenches were literally crammed with corpses, so much so that our infantry men could not make any use of them. Violent counter attacks were broken, and only served to increase the enemy's losses.

MAISONS-DE-CHAMPAGNE was the scene of heavy battles during the attack of September 25, 1915. Here our troops captured more than 20 German guns, courageously defended by their personnel.

BUTTE-DU-MESNIL.—Our troops met, on September 25, with a stubborn resistance near the borders of this place. Two squadrons of Hussars charged with drawn swords on the bastion, the centre of the defence, and got hold of it ; taking in addition 600 prisoners.

FERME DE NAVARIN.—The Farm of Navarin could not be taken in our first onset of September 25, 1915. It was conquered by our troops on October 6, 1915. The preparatory bombardment had been a fearful one ; the German wounded could not be evacuated on account of our curtain fire on the roads of communication.

For four days the Germans had nothing to drink, nevertheless they resisted hardily. In the end, 480 men and 10 officers, all that was left of the regiment in charge of the position, were forced to surrender.

BUTTE DE TAHURE.—On September 25, 1915, we had got hold of the hill slopes, but had not been able to take the ridge. On September 28 a regiment succeeded at night in advancing quite close to the enemy. The colonel, two commanders of the battalion and the ensign were killed by the same shell ; the surviving officer took the command of the regiment, the flag was raised and a trench dug under the fire of the enemy machine guns ; this trench was to be used for the next morning's attack. Once the ridge was taken, the village offered but a very slight resistance. To the south of Tahure, the Germans, however, had organised the trenches with seven parallel lines echeloned behind each other to a depth of three kilomètres. Tahure and its environs were taken by the Foreign Legion.

THE MASSIF OF MORONVILLIERS consists of a series of ridges about 600 ft. high, and stretches from Dontrien to Nauroy.

From East to West are famous positions like Mont-sans-Nom, Le Téton, Le Mont-Haut, Le Casque, Le Cornillet.

Our attack was launched on the south of the Chemin-des-Dames on April 16, 1917, and extended the next morning to the sector on the right of Reims. Our troops tried to take the whole line of hills. The first onslaught gained us the possession of the greater part of the crests, but a few having successfully resisted the assault, it was necessary to engage in extremely violent local combats, and only after several days of terrible fighting the position fell into our hands. The Germans attempted numerous counter-attacks, but none of them could secure finally the possession of one of the famous ridges. The attacking army commanded by General Anthoine made 5,000 prisoners, 50 guns, and deprived the enemy of a first-class observation post. The Massif of Moronvilliers was perforce abandoned by General Gouraud at the time of the German offensive on July 15, 1918, but was soon after retaken.

The Germans had dug under Mount Cornillet a vast tunnel, able to hold nearly three battalions. During the artillery preparation on April 17, 1917, one of our big shells happened to break into the ventilation chimney of a dug-out. Ammunition had been stored in the galleries, so that everything was blown up by the explosion, and the tunnel became a fearful slaughterhouse where a few wounded tried to free themselves from the 700 corpses heaped up in the narrow galleries.

REIMS.—The Germans penetrated this city on September 4, 1914, after a preliminary bombardment which killed 60 civilians. On the 12th, at night, the French recaptured the town, and on the 17th a few German batteries established at Nogent-l'Abbesse, began to bombard the

Ph. Lévy

REIMS. Saint Remy Church

cathedral, causing some slight damage. The German wounded had
been transported into the Cathedral and the enemy informed of it.
Nevertheless, the cathedral was continually the object of his cannonading, so that on the 18th it was hit by some 220 incendiary shells.
The soldiers and civilians, amongst whom was Cardinal Lucon, Archbishop of Reims, devoted themselves to saving from the fire the
unfortunate German wounded, but, in spite of their humanity, 63 of the
injured perished, victims of their own countrymen's barbarism.

Ph. Lévy

REIMS. Town Hall

Ph. Neurdein

REIMS. The Cathedral

The bombardment of Reims continued the whole year. Each military check the Germans suffered was a pretext for setting on fire and destroying a few more blocks of houses. In 1918 there were still several thousands of civilians left in the city, but the military authorities forced them to leave the town. Cardinal Lucon was the last man to leave.

At the time of their offensive on May 27, 1918, the Germans tried once more to get hold of Reims, but they succeeded only in approaching the Western outskirts. Another big effort was attempted on July 15. Reims was then entirely encircled. We reacted immediately, however, and from July 20 to 30 the enemy was driven from the buttresses of the "Montagne de Reims," where he had succeeded in establishing himself. Fierce combats took place south-east of Reims towards Sainte-Euphrasie, Vrigny, and Bligny, where, side by side, several American divisions and Italian army corps scored great successes. Little by little the town was regained, and at last the enemy lost all hope of capturing it. In vain he coveted it, in vain he took revenge for the losses he suffered by incessantly bombarding Reims and her beautiful cathedral.

FORT OF BRIMONT.—It was from this fort that the Germans bombarded Reims during practically the whole war. A big effort was made by us on April 16, 1917, to get hold of it. The Russian troops of the French front co-operated valiantly with this attack, and we succeeded in getting the lower part of the ridge, but it was impossible to take the work itself.

NOGENT-L'ABBESSE.—It was here that the first German batteries were established, firing on Reims. From 1915 we tried several times vainly to secure this strong position; a new effort in April, 1917, was equally without result.

REIMS CATHEDRAL

The world learned with profound sorrow that the Germans had set on fire Reims Cathedral, and that their sacrilegious shells obstinately attempted to destroy this jewel of French art. "One felt," wrote Mr. E. Male, "that a star was on the wane and that beauty had diminished on earth."

Our Lady of Reims was one of those masterpieces of art wherein not only a nation but the whole human race could admire itself. It was, in the sphere of architectural beauty, like a realised ideal. The Cathedral of Chartres gives chiefly an impression of force. Our Lady of Paris, a little dark, is obscured with a mantle of mystery; the Cathedral of Reims, with its slender nave, its wide, stained-glass windows, its roses, appeared as if radiating light, all grace and force, all grandeur and beauty; her walls were singing the joy, the love and hallelujah of victory.

The construction of Reims Cathedral was undertaken in 1212 and continued until the fourteenth century. The name of the architect has up to now remained unknown. His name has been found recently ; it is to Jean d'Orbais that we owe the plan of the " Cathedral of the Angels."

Ph. Neurdein

REIMS. Interior of the Cathedral

Notre Dame de Reims was one of the most spacious cathedrals of France ; it measured 420 ft. in length, over 90 ft. in width, its vaults rose to a height of 111 ft. The proportions were marvellously calculated, the nave, narrower than that of Chartres, seemed by this very fact to be much more slender. The small columns, the Gothic arches, and the bands of the vaults ascended with an incomparable grace and lightness. The Reims architect had not only the admirable logic of the Greek masters, he had the soul of a poet. The mullioned windows,

59

the worked-out capitals, and numerous high reliefs decorated the choir, the two transepts and the nave of the Cathedral.

All this interior, admirable in the proportions of its large lines, in the beauty and the finish of its details, was adorned with magnificent coloured windows. Time, and the development of a special flora, had darkened the luminous masterpieces of the Reims glass-makers. They had acquired a great richness of tone. What now remain are only heaps of formless lead strips and rubbish of coloured glass.

The harmony of the great lines, the lightness and the boldness of the Gothic arches, and the richness of the sculpture which characterises the interior of the Cathedral are found also on the outside.

Ph. Neurdein

REIMS. Statues of the Great Portal of the Cathedral

The Reims buttresses are marvels of a charming art which had known how to clothe with grace and beauty such elements of architecture whose part is but an indispensable support for the vaults.

The façade was a pure wonder. Less rigid than that of Chartres, or of Notre Dame de Paris, it appeared full of life and grace, lightness and ease : with its slender Gothic arches, its rosace as delicate as Flanders lace, its little bells chiselled like women's jewels and its two towers thrown against heaven like an aspiration.

Innumerable bas-reliefs, thousands of statues, embellished the five front doors of the admirable basilica ; the whole Bible was represented there, and the people saw living again in the stone the episodes of the Old and New Testaments.

The statues of the façade, carved at the end of the thirteenth century, are intrinsic masterpieces. The central front door is entirely consecrated to Our Lady, and it is the very sweetness, beauty, and grace of the Virgin which appear on all these stone figures. The scenes of the Lady Day and the Visitation, the bas-relief of the last Judgment, have always been admired by visitors. The "Smile of Reims," an angel with his face enlightened by a heavenly joy, his body delicately inclined in a delightful posture, was famous throughout the whole world. The statues of the side entrance doors, more ancient, are as old as the beginning of the thirteenth century. They have still the stiffness and the majestic rigidness of the Chartres statues. They do not give impression of life, as the statues of the central door entrance, but an impression of calmness, restful-

Ph. Neurdein

REIMS. Statues of the Great Portal of the Cathedral

ness, of meditative grandeur : one would think they had been taken from ancient Egypt.

Now all this is over, the nave is crushed down, the statues are destroyed or lie mutilated in the Cathedral's crypt. Blackened, torn to pieces, tottering, the fine stone laces have lost something of their grace and beauty. Before such a disaster one begins to cry ; cursing the Vandals who have destroyed such masterpieces ; one fears to touch such open wounds. Yet can one leave what is still left of this marvel a prey to time ? These ruins speak still of what the Cathedral was : if one does not take care, what has been the pride of the whole nation, of a whole civilisation, will be only a heap of formless rubbish. The Cathedral of Reims must be built again. Even if imperfectly rebuilt, a restoration will preserve something of the grace and beauty of the antique monument.

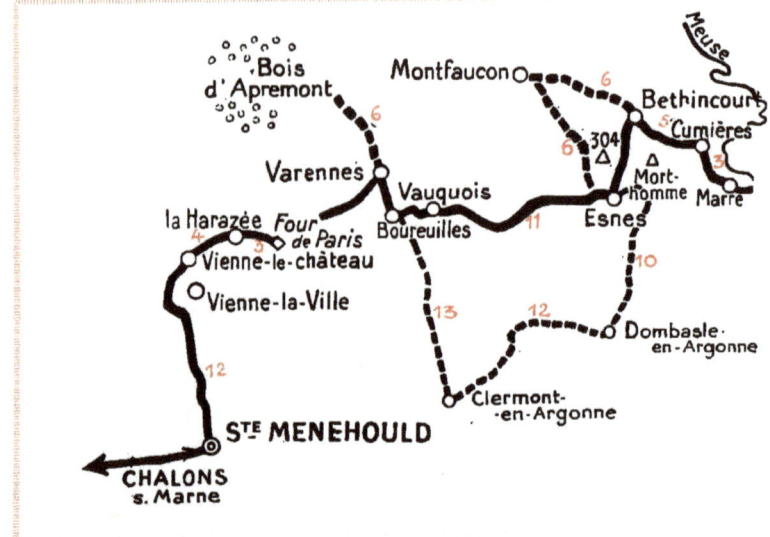

Sector 3—Verdun
Route

From *Châlons* the tourist will reach rapidly *Sainte-Ménehould*. After a quick visit to this little town, he will take the road of *Vienne-le-Château*, and after having left this place and the village of *La Harazée* he will stop at the famous crossing-point of the *Four-de-Paris*; then he will continue his route till *Varennes*.

From Varennes he may go up to the woods of *Apremont*. Back to Varennes, he may, after the visit to *Vauquois*, go down to *Clermont-en-Argonne* and reach *Esnes* through *Dombasle-en-Argonne*, or go straight from Varennes to *Esnes* through *Avocourt*.

From Esnes he may go to visit *Montfaucon*, and from there go to *Bethincourt*; he will see on his left the ridge 304.

From Bethincourt reach *Cumières*. On the right of the route is the *Mort-Homme*. From Cumières reach the *Meuse* through *Marre*, cross the river at *Charny*. From *Bras* go to *Vacherauville*, and from Vacherauville to *Beaumont*, then, on the right, one has the hill of *Poivre*. Before reaching Beaumont a little dash to the north will allow one to see the wood of *Caures*. From Beaumont get down to *Douaumont* and the Fort of Douaumont through *Louvemont*.

From Douaumont, descend down to *Vaux*, to climb afterwards to the Fort of Vaux, and then looking on *Verdun* one will have on one's right the *Butte of Thiaumont*, *Froideterre* and *Fleury*; on one's left *Damloup*. From Vaux reach *Verdun*. It is not possible now to get by automobile either to Fleury or to the Fort of Souville.

From Verdun, take the route of Metz, turn to the right in front of the fort of *Rozellier*. Follow the route till *Eparges*, visit the Eparges. Take again the road and turn to the right at the height of *Vieville-les-Côtes*, then run on to *Dompierre-aux-Bois*. At *Seuzey* one will cross the ancient lines.

At *Lacroix-sur-Meuse* turn to the left, take the road of *Saint-Mihiel*. After the visit to this town take the road of *Apremont*, visit the Forest, then run on to *Flirey*. Seicheprey is on the left.

At Flirey, turn to the right and follow the high road to *Toul*, and from Toul reach *Nancy*.

|||||||||||||||||||||||||||||||||||||||||||||||||||||||||||||||||||||||||||||||||||||||||||||||||||||||||||||||||

HOTELS

BAR-LE-DUC

GRAND HOTEL DU COMMERCE.   50 rooms. Electric Lighting.
Boulevard de la Rochelle.   Central heating. Modern
Telephone 110.   comfort. Garage.

SAINTE-MENEHOULD

HOTEL DE METZ.   30 rooms. Modern comfort.
33 Rue Chanzy.   Auto-garage.
Bertault, owner.

TOUL

HOTEL DE METZ.   Modern comfort. Garage.
18 Rue Gambetta.
Telephone 79.

VERDUN

HOTEL DU COQ HARDI.   Comfort. Garage.
Rue du Saint-Esprit.
owner, L. Bellot.

Historical Account

Verdun owns a certain number of interesting historical relics; the Cathedral, the Bishopric, the Porte-Chaussée, which is also a prison. In 1792 Verdun was besieged by the Prussians. Her defender, Beaurepaire, seeing himself forced to surrender, shot himself. In 1870, Verdun resisted heavy attacks for more than a month.

Varennes-en-Argonne has remained famous for the arrest of Louis XVI in his flight on June 21, 1791.

Industrial Account

The region of the Meuse is composed of calcareous plateaux cut up by the flow of the Meuse, and of the few tributaries flowing into it at the right and left. The population is mainly agricultural, the valleys alone are fertile, and there various kinds of corn are cultivated; on the hills grow the vine producing the famous grey wines of the Meuse, and on the plateaux there are numerous forests. There is little or no industrial activity—only a few iron-works and engineering-shops at Bar-le-Duc and at Verdun.

The manufacture of sweetmeats occupies a certain number of workmen in this region. Verdun was famous for its sugar-plums, Stenay and Commercy for their pastries (madeleines and biscuits).

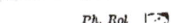

Ph. Rol

Gen. SARRAIL

Ph. Rol

Marshal PETAIN

Ph. Rol

Gen. GUILLAUMAT

Ph. Meley

Gen. NIVELLE

Short Account of the Operations

" **VERDUN.**" This word alone suffices to evoke the image of the French Army, erect in front of the enemy, standing with breast bruised by a thousand strokes, scarred and wounded, defiantly shouting, " Thou shalt not pass ! "

The battle of Verdun was a series of extremely violent local fights, which, from February 1916 to 1918, stained with blood the hills at the right and at the left, of the Hauts-de-Meuse to the east ; and up to the Argonne Forest to the west. The Germans only developed the tactics we had employed in the Champagne (September, 1915). They preceded their attacks by long and violent bombardments, and rushed to the onslaught only when their artillery fire had destroyed all the French organisations and reduced the number of the defenders considerably. Their objectives were always very limited ; a village, a ridge, and some-times a trench line. Around such an objective, wrecked by the heavy artillery, they created a " death zone," by means of curtain fire of the 77's and poison shells, so as to prevent our reinforcements reaching the threatened position. On our side the artillery sought to shell principally the German concentration centres, in order to throw panic and death among the troops which were preparing to attack. Our curtain fire killed hundreds of thousands of Germans, and when we were supplied with heavy long range artillery, our 240's, 380's and the 400's retaliated against the German batteries and destroyed a good number of them. As to our infantry, often, in the centre of resistance, all that was left was a handful of heroes whom the noble folly of their duty exalted. They resisted the enemy's attack, frequently out-numbered one against ten, fighting only with their gun or grenade, often with their bayonet or knife. They submitted to be killed, but not

65

E

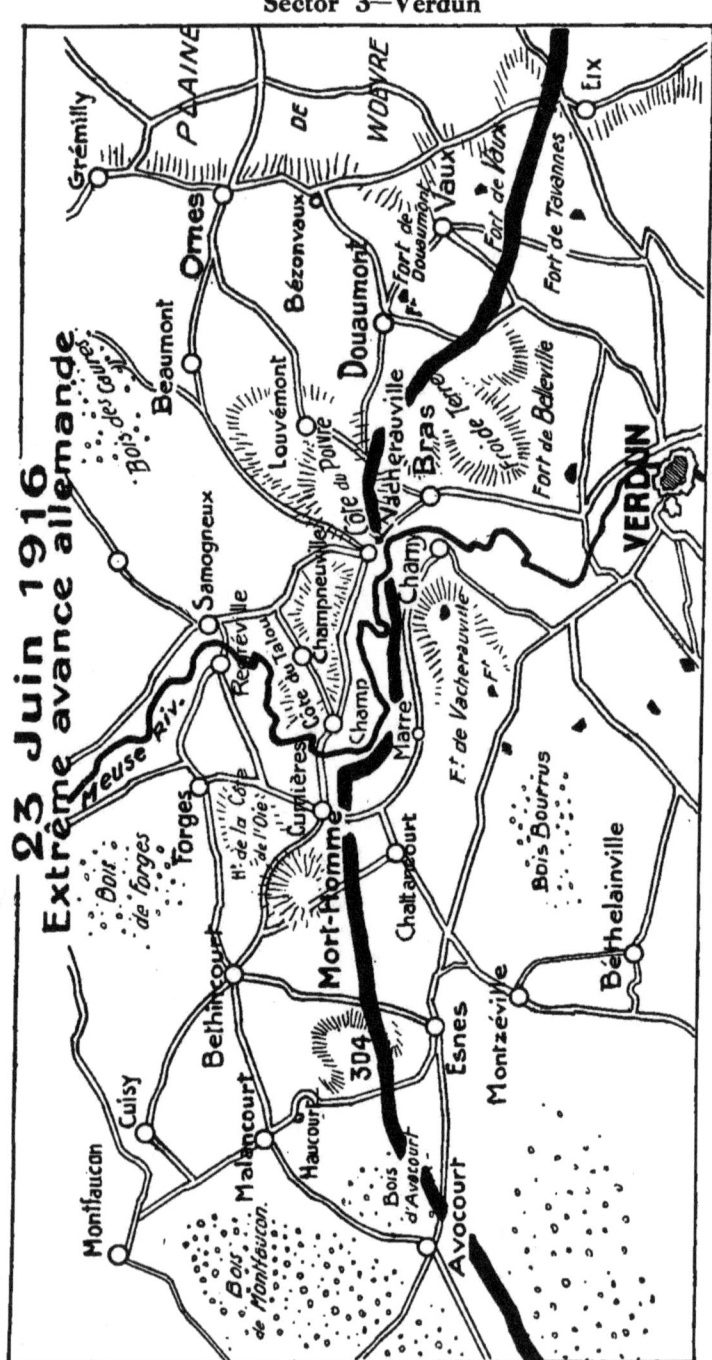

23 Juin 1916 — Extrême avance allemande

CHAMP DE BATAILLE DE VERDUN

one soldier withdrew, and if sometimes they were encircled and forced to surrender, it was only after they had defended themselves like lions.

The German attack was launched on February 21, 1916, after a fearful bombardment which lasted several days. The sector had remained very calm up to that time, our troops were not numerous. Before the tremendous push of the enemy they had to withdraw, but defended the ground foot by foot, incessantly counter-attacking. For several days Verdun was considered certain to fall. Then our reinforced troops offered suddenly an obstinate resistance. The German attacks, though repeated every day with more violence, no longer succeeded in pressing our soldiers back.

The battle continued ruthlessly in March and April; at the beginning of June the Germans made a renewed effort, and gained the Fort of Vaux, but no strategic advantage.

On October 24, 1916, our troops, in their turn, took the offensive and progressed as far as the Fort of Douaumont. At the commencement of November they attacked again and occupied the Fort of Vaux. On September 13, a new victorious offensive brought us to the Woods of Caurrieres. In July, 1917, we were attacking to the East of the Meuse and won splendid victories in the sector of Avocourt. Verdun was definitely released. The fighting in this sector, where so much blood had been shed, suddenly ceased. It began again at the end of September, 1918. The American Army, with an irresistable impetus, carried their line further, and progressed up to Consenvoye, Dun-sur-Meuse and Stenay.

A few figures will give an idea of the enormous expenditure of shells made by the Germans at the time of their attacks of 1916. During the bombardment on February 21, 1916, preparatory to the initial attack, 80,000 shells of .210 and .305 were fired on a front of but one kilometre wide and 1,200 ft. deep. In order to prepare their attack on June 22 the Germans threw on Froideterre, Souville, Fleury, and the ravines more than 200,000 asphyxiating shells.

At Verdun, the French Army won the admiration of the world. Millions of German soldiers were thrown into this furnace. 700,000 men were sacrificed by the Crown Prince for the satisfaction of the Germanic pride, without having attained any appreciable result after ten months of stubborn fighting. When it pleased their commanders, the same army which had sustained the frightful shock of the German masses took back in a few days the ground which these masses had only won in four months, fighting foot by foot at the price of enormous losses.

At the time of the German offensive on Verdun, this sector was commanded by General Herr, but on February 25 he was replaced by General Petain, who within eight days restored the previously critical situation, assured France that Verdun would not be taken and issued his famous promise: " On les aura " (We'll have them). General Nivelle distinguished himself in this sector in the successful offensives of October and November, 1916. Later on, General Guillaumat, and afterwards General Hirschauer, took the command of the Army of Verdun, which had now become the second Army. More than one commander achieved at Verdun a lasting and immortal glory. Our victory, however, is due more, perhaps, to the spirit of sacrifice and to the heroism of the fighters than to the brilliant manœuvres. On the German side it was the Crown Prince who directed the attack of his troops, a nominal command, as the Imperial Prince soon left Charleville, where he had led the life of a debauchee.

War Facts

BOIS D'APREMONT was one of the most bloody sectors of the front. There were no important offensives but a perpetual fighting between the trenches, numerous raids and a subterranean activity which lasted for a long while.

VAUQUOIS.—The Eperon de Vauquois (the spur of Vauquois which the enemy possessed ever since 1914) constituted an excellent observation post, allowing him to direct the fire of his guns advantageously on to our lines of communication. On February 17, 1915, a strong attack carried our troops from the Marshes where they were established at the foot of the ridge, to the slopes of the Eperon. On the 28th a new attack brought us to the border of the plateau, but we did not succeed in capturing the village. The battle for Vauquois lasted until March 5. In the cemetery struggles took place, of a bitterness and violence which was previously unequalled. Finally on the 5th a French soldier hoisted the tri-colour on the summit of the ruins of the ancient church.

MONTFAUCON.—Is built on a height which dominates all the regions to the west of the Meuse. Formerly, on this ridge there was a fine fortress, of which now nothing remains but the ruins. From nearly all the points of the Verdun sector one could see l'aiguille de Montfaucon ("needle of Montfaucon"). For this reason it was an excellent point of observation for the enemy, permitted him to survey all our movements in the Verdun area, and to facilitate the accurate direction of the fire of his heavy artillery on our concentration camps and roads of access.

Montfaucon was taken by the American army in its offensive of September 26, on the right and on the left banks of the Meuse, an offensive which eventually resulted in the capture of 8,000 prisoners and 100 guns.

CLERMONT-EN-ARGONNE was looted in 1914 by the German army, and afterwards suffered from the long-range bombardments which the Germans undertook in 1916 and 1917. Their heavy guns made a particular mark of the important line Sainte-Menehould-Verdun.

Sector 3—Verdun

DOMBASLE-EN-ARGONNE underwent the same fate as Clermont. One will notice near the station, on a concrete water basin, the curious effect produced by the explosion of a shell in the middle of the liquid mass.

BOIS D'AVOCOURT was taken by the Germans on March 20, 1916, after an attack with poison gas and liquid fire. A colonel refused to abandon his post of command, and continued to inform the reserve of the movements of the enemy until the very moment they arrived : " Here they are," were his last words. On the 29th, the Germans delivered another attack, but did not succeed in debouching from the woods. The Colonel of a French regiment was killed in this second attack, and his son, in the course of the combat, found him lying at the bottom of a ravine ; he kissed him on the forehead and went to resume his place at the head of his section. Avocourt was recaptured by us on August 20, 1917, in three-quarters of an hour, and almost without any losses. That day our offensive had extended to the whole sector of the left bank of the Meuse, and our soldiers took 5,000 prisoners.

COTE 304.—The ridge 304 was one of the most dubious positions of the Battle of Verdun. It was the scene of obstinate hand-to-hand fighting. On May 20 the enemy launched an extremely violent attack in this sector. More than 20,000 Germans essayed to climb the slopes of the Mort-Homme and the Cote 304 ; 15,000 corpses were heaped up on this shattered ground without producing any impression on our lines. A Major, who had had his shoulder smashed, took part in a counter-attack at the head of his battalion, and, again wounded, while they were dressing the injury, he sang the " Marseillaise."

MORT-HOMME (Dead Man) owes its name to a cross raised on the spot where was once found the corpse of a murdered traveller. The fight on the Mort-Homme has known the same phases as at the Cote 304. On May 6 the Germans concentrated the fire-power of 80 batteries against the Mort-Homme. On May 22 their infantry stormed several times, but each time the heroism of our soldiers broke their waves. Nevertheless, Mort-Homme fell into the hands of the Germans at the end of the day, but was retaken on August 21 at the same time as Avocourt.

LA COTE DU POIVRE was the scene of some of the most furious contests in the Verdun sector. It witnessed a thousand deeds of heroism. We will cite just one. A German shell had killed the loader of a machine gun and broken the gun carriage. Arrived at the firing position, the gunner asks for a volunteer to sustain it. A young soldier, recently arrived at the front, offers himself, and the gunner, having placed the weapon on his shoulder, begins to fire from this human support. Though his shoulder was bruised and half burnt, the heroic volunteer did not cease to fulfil his part until the German attack was broken.

69

Ph. Meuriess.

Col. DRIANT

BOIS DES CAURES.—It was from the north edge of the wood of Caures that the German attack on February 21 issued. The wood, practically obliterated by the shells, was taken the next day. Lieut.-Colonel Driant at the head of his chasseurs instantly counter-attacked, and succeeded in retaking the southern part of the wood, in the course of which he met with a glorious death.

THIAUMONT.—The hills of Thiaumont and Fleur were always coveted by the Germans, who continually sought to get hold of them. The most violent attack was that of June 22, 1916, 200,000 asphyxiating shells were thrown against the sector of Thiaumont-Fleury-Souville ; nineteen regiments rushed to the onslaught, Thiaumont itself was taken by the Bavarians, not without frightful losses. The enemy failed before Souville, repelled by our machine guns. On July 30 a brilliantly directed attack gave us back Thiaumont.

DOUAUMONT.—The village and the fort of Douaumont were the scenes of many hard battles. The village was taken by the Germans several times, and each time reconquered by our vigorous counter-attack. The 24th Brandenburgers got hold of the fort the first time on February 24, 1916 ; the German wireless announced this victory to the whole world. This attack had taken place in the morning, and at 2 p.m. the French Iron Division counter-attacked, and succeeded in regaining the position. The enemy only abandoned it foot by foot. It was again assaulted and lost to us the same day. On May 22 the division of General Mangin rushed to attack the fort. Within eleven minutes, three lines of trenches were crossed and the desired objective taken. During the 22nd and 23rd we held the position in spite of violent counter-attacks ; on the 24th we had to yield, under the pressure of a whole Bavarian army corps.

Douaumont and the fort of Douaumont were retaken in one rush at the time of our offensive on October 24, to the right of the Meuse. The movement was carried out under a heavy rain, on wet ground, but, nevertheless, was followed by a complete success. A colonial battalion took the fort of Douaumont in presence of generals Joffre and Petain.

THE FORT OF VAUX.—In the month of June 1916 the Germans made a terrific effort to get hold of the Fort of Vaux. It was there that one of the most characteristic episodes of the battle of Verdun took place. Since June 2, the battle was waged round the fort itself, partially invested by the enemy. Major Raynal was imprisoned underground with 600 battle-weary men, with hardly any ammunition, and without water. On the 3rd and 4th Vaux is still resisting, but all communica-

tions are cut. On the 5th two men succeed
in getting through, and by various signals
they re-establish the liasion. Nothing
could be more dramatic than the supreme
appeals sent forth from the fort of Vaux.
" The enemy is preparing a mining-gallery
to blow up the vault, let him have it with
your artillery. We are attacked by gases
and liquid fire. We are exhausted." From
our lines they answer that a counter-attack
is in readiness, but it was found impossible
to debouch from cover, and, in the evening,
Major Raynal, at the end of his resources, had to surrender.

Ph. Meurisse

Comdt. RAYNAL

One shudders to think of the suffering which, during this awfu
period the defenders of Vaux had to endure. These men were fighting
for a whole week, for four days they were burning with an ardent thirst,
they had to fight with grenades, they had to dig, to re-establish their
casemates and trenches under a frightful concentration fire, in an
atmosphere infected with asphyxiating gases. The enemy himself,
moved by such bravery, allowed Major Raynal to keep his sword, and
military honours were paid to the heroic garrison.

The Fort of Vaux was retaken without a shot. On November 21,
1916, having sustained for a few days a heavy bombardment, the
Germans evacuated the fort, and our patrols entered it without striking
a blow.

Verdun is one of the frontier towns which has most suffered from
the war, though the Germans were never able to capture it. They
took revenge for their continual defeats by incessantly bombarding
the town with their long range howitzers. The few historic monuments the town once possessed are now ruined.

The inhabitants of Verdun were hastily withdrawn the evening
before the first German attack on February 21, 1916. Very few found
their houses uninjured on their return.

The town of Verdun, inasmuch as it personifies the heroic resistance
of our soldiers in this sector, has been decorated with the Cross of the
Legion d'Honneur and numerous crosses of foreign orders.

A Vision of the Battlefield

The tourist, having gone through the battlefields, should stop at
the Fort of Vaux. On turning to the north-west he will see on the
right the immense plain of the Woevre, and far off the white silhouette
of Etain in ruins, and behind, the high chimneys of Conflans and
Audun-le-Roman. A little more to the north the horizon is bounded
by a range of hills on which Villerupt and Longwy are situated. In
front of him is the fort of Douaumont, concealing from view the Cote

du Poivre and the Cote de Talous ; a little to the left the plateau of Thiaumont, then Fleury, at last, directly on his right, Souville ; at his back, the fort of Tavennes.

In order to help the traveller to understand exactly how this battle appeared, we give here a description written by an officer who served the whole month of May 1916 in the Fort of Vaux.

" From the observation post of Vaux, I see nearly all the battlefield to the east of the Meuse. There exist no words with which to describe the strange sensation of death and destruction one feels in the face of this spectacle, which seems not of this world, but of some infernal region. All around me, a series of hills or rather of enormous heaps of yellowish earth, are scattered, each encroaching on and entangling itself with its neighbour. No trace of greenness, no tree, not one blade

Ph. Lévy

VERDUN. Panorama of the Meuse

of grass on all these hills, whose soil, composed of holes swollen and scooped up by the shells, seems out of the twisted arms made by a few torn and blackened trees to show to heaven its open bowels cut to pieces by the iron and fire.

Between these hills, above the dark and gloomy ravines, hover yellowish clouds of some noxious gas, and one would say they resemble a shadow of death, ever embracing the few living men who still attempt to point a gun ; far away on the hills of Douaumont and Thiaumont grey ghosts seem to crawl over this shattered earth ; these are our first lines.

" Suddenly a line of white smoke-wreaths is observed on the crest of a hill, a dull roll is heard ; this is the curtain fire launched by the Germans, and which precedes a fearful bombardment. The heavy

Ph. Lévy

VERDUN. The Cathedral

batteries begin their action, and down there, there is an immense rumbling heard, which, in turn, increases and fades away.

"Above our heads the great shells pass, carrying their inevitable message behind us; the 75's are in action, constantly speeding up their jerky strokes. Everywhere, on the hills, in the valleys, the shells tear up the soil, a white stain, some earth, wood-rubbish, often a bundle of human limbs becomes visible, then a white or yellow cloud arises, forms itself into a long trail of smoke, and slowly mounts into

Ph. Lévy

VERDUN. Fifteenth Century Gate

the atmosphere which eventually obscures it. One would think oneself in the middle of a collection of volcanoes, emitting their fumes through thousands of open craters on their summits and flanks.

"Down there, a thick greenish cloud is rolling heavily along the bottom of a ravine. This is the deadly gas. Near us unexploded shells frequently fall; they are smashed noiselessly, and the fearful vapour that issues brings with it the odour of mortification. The machine guns are crackling, subside for a little while, then they start again. What is happening? Down there a line of grey shadows advance, another follows, then another, and finally a confused mass. The enemy is attacking, the firing redoubles, the mass of fighters loses itself in the smoke of the shells and of the grenades, and always round it rages the bombardment. Has he taken the trench he is coveting? How many of our men are fallen there? We do not know, we shall not know. One does not know anything of each other at 1 kilometre distance. Sometimes not at 1,500 or even 600 ft. In this narrow space where thousands and thousands of men are moving one feels oneself isolated, prostrated, lost in the infernal chaos.

"The bombardment suddenly loses something of its intensity, the machine guns no longer ceaselessly cause their deadly yelping to be heard. The attack has ended; it will, no doubt, be recommenced this evening. Here? There? On us? We do not know. The night may come without the fight having terminated. The shining fuses will trace in the darkness their stripes of mournful fire, in the valley shadows will move about; relief troops, stretcher bearers, toilers of every sort, but the German cannon will not interrupt punctuating with red marks like blood-stains the heavy vale of darkness and of death. And day succeeds day amidst this desolation in this living hell.

"On my right, in the ravine of death, a few batteries lie cut to pieces by the Germans' 210's: the swollen horses, enormous as they seem, are stretching towards heaven their stiffened feet. On the caissons, on the overturned cannons, on the ground, are extended human corpses whose faces and hands, made white through death, contrast violently with the dark colour of their cloaks. A yellowish water is dripping in the shell holes about this debris of corpses, and a thirsty wounded man is drinking of this frightful water.

"We must have rooted in our hearts I do not know what folly, what kind of fanaticism in our love for our country, in order to be inspired with the wild determination which is keeping us here: ' You must not yield, the enemy shall not have Verdun, you must oppose your naked breast to the blows of the German, but shall not retreat.'"

Supply Service to the Battlefields

From the first days of the offensive the railroad which connected Bar-le-Duc with Verdun was captured, under the fire of the German guns. The trains coming from Sainte-Menehould were not able to go

further than Clermont-en-Argonne
by any other route. It was, there-
fore, necessary to secure, by means of motor cars, the supply of men,
ammunition and foods for our soldiers in the terrible battle. The
route of Bar-le-Duc to Verdun through Souilly was the main route
followed by thousands and thousands of motor cars. The heavy
lorries followed each other without interruption in a long line, but every
600 or 900 ft. they left a certain distance free in order that the Head-
quarter's cars might pass. On certain days two convoys went by
parallel roads, so the circulation was made only in one way ; returning
they took other parallel roads. At all times, men of the engineering
corps were at work repairing the roads, which were rapidly used up by
the excellent solid tyres with which our heavy lorries were provided.

If the French Army held out at Verdun one and a half years against
the most tremendous efforts of an enemy, determined to conquer, she
owes this partially to the motor-car section, whose incessant efforts
succeeded in securing her supplies. The drivers were continually on
their vehicles. There were two on each lorry and whilst the one slept
the other drove, and if the latter felt his moral force abandon him and
his eyes close in spite of himself, he would wake his companion, who
would take his place at the steering wheel.

The route from Bar-le-Duc to Verdun received the name of " the
sacred road," for she saw thousands and thousands of heroes passing
up to the battle, animated by an invincible ardour, and coming back
shattered and maimed, covered with an immortal glory.

The Salient of **SAINT-MIHIEL.**—From Verdun, to be exact, from
Fresnes to Pont-à-Mousson, the German line had the shape of a wedge,
of which Saint-Mihiel was a point. This extremely hilly region is
covered with numerous woods, of which a few were the scene of a
fearful trench warfare. Many efforts were attempted on our side to
break through the " Hernie of Saint-Mihiel," to the north in the woods
of Eparges, to the south in the woods of Apremont and Bois-le-Prêtre.
In face of the many facilities which this position afforded the enemy
we were forced to undertake a real siege war where progress was only
possible by mining from trench to trench, and by raids. The Germans

opposed an obstinate resistance, and the fight having become very desperate and without any strategic result, the high command gave up this mine war and the sector became comparatively calm.

On September 13, 1918, the Americans went on with the fighting, and by a splendid assault took the salient of Saint-Mihiel, making 15,000 prisoners, comprising nearly a whole Austrian division, in three days ; 200 big guns were also among the trophies. It was a great victory for the American Army. The tanks performed marvellous feats. A sergeant alone on board a small tank captured 75 prisoners and several guns. The American cavalry could at last be utilised and made good use of their opportunity.

LES EPARGES.—Quite a series of small operations were carried out on the various parts of this sector and all were alike. Here is an example : at the Eparges the Germans had built a strong redoubt, and we made it the chief objective of our attack. After careful preparation, by means of sapping and mining and sustained artillery fire, we took this redoubt by a brilliant assault. It was afterwards again lost, but two days later we captured it once more. For a whole week they were fighting still on the same ground or on its immediate environs, and then the fighting began in another place, sometimes for the possession of a ridge, or a bastion, and sometimes for a simple trench element.

The underground contest was particularly heavy at the Eparges. The two lines were very close. French and Germans sought reciprocally to demolish their opponent's defences. An underground sap, like a very narrow gallery, was tunnelled from our line, until it was under the enemy's trench or under a German bastion. They would heap up an enormous quantity of gunpowder. Our troops would retreat slightly, and by means of Bickford cord or an electric detonator they then caused the explosion of the mine.

As soon as the rock boulders thrown up by the explosion had subsided, a small group of attacking men would rush forward to occupy the crater. Around these craters, measuring sometimes a diameter of 120 to 150 ft. and a depth of 30 to 60, many stubborn engagements with the gun, bayonet, grenade and knife have taken place.

The Germans employed the same method. Special listening posts were established for the purpose of taking by surprise their mine operations.

As soon as a sap was discovered, a sloping gallery was started for the purpose of disposing a mine chimney near the sap and so blocking it up. This counter-mine was commonly known as a camouflet.

SAINT-MIHIEL.—At the end of 1914 we attempted to take Saint-Mihiel by surprise. Our troops rushed up on to the barracks of Chauvoncourt, but the Germans having been previously informed of it, had evacuated them so that when our soldiers penetrated there, the ground, already carefully undermined, was blown up under their feet and the whole detachment perished in that trap.

In the beginning of September, 1918, General Pershing was determined to reduce the Salient of Saint-Mihiel. He would attack it both North and South so as, in effect, to strangle it between the pincers. The Germans being warned of it began to fall back, but on the 12th the Americans inaugurated their attack and rushed on so rapidly that the Germans had scarcely time to retire. They had just begun to loot the town. In face of the danger of a bloodless capture they had to forsake the congenial occupation, hurriedly leaving the railway trucks full of stolen goods. Most of the inhabitants had remained in St. Mihiel, and it was with an indescribable joy that they welcomed the American soldiers who had come to deliver them from the German yoke.

TROYON.—The fort underwent a heavy fire of big mortars on September 8, 1914. A German officer, preceded by a white flag, then presented himself at the entrance. Summoned the first time to surrender, the commanding officer answered, "Never"; the second time: "France entrusted me with the guard of the fort, I would rather shoot myself than surrender." Finally, the third time, "Go away from here, I have seen enough of you." As soon as the deputy had left, the bombardment was recommenced with redoubled violence. A division from Toul delivered it the next morning; the fort was half ruined, but it had definitely forbidden the enemy the access to the Meuse.

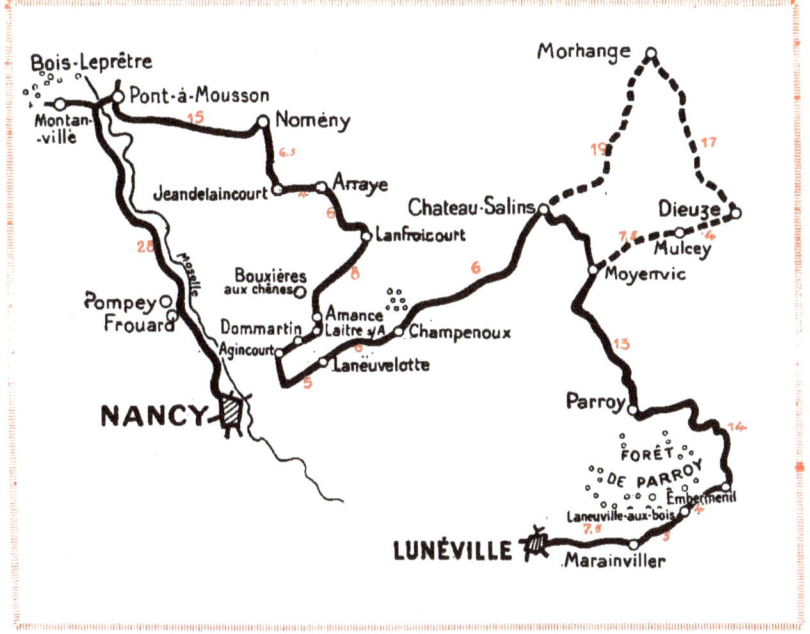

Sector 4—Nancy

Route

From *Nancy* take the *Metz* route and drive to *Pont-à-Mousson*, and note in passing the factories of *Frouard* and *Pompey*.

At Pont-à-Mousson you may turn to the left, take the road of *Montanville*, and visit *Bois-le-Prêtre*, or cross the *Moselle* and drive to *Nomeny*.

From Nomeny descend to *Jeandelaincourt*, turn to the left, drive on to *Arrey*, the road turns to the south at *Lanfroicourt*, retake the road of Nancy until opposite *Bouxières-aux-Chênes*, there turn to the left, pass to *Amance*, *Laitre-sous-Amance*, *Donmartin*, *Agincourt*, there turn to the left. At the main road of *Nancy-Dieuze* turn once more to the left. After *Laneuvelotte* one will see on the left the woods of *Champenoux* (do not visit it, there is nothing left of the battle).

Two miles past the old frontier turn to the left and visit *Chateau-Salins*.

From Chateau-Salins you may go to *Morhange*; then return through *Dieuze*, *Mulcey* and *Moyen-Vic*, from there follow the frontier, which was approximately the front line, circle the woods of *Parroy*, visit *Embermenil*, then *Laneuville-aux-Bois*, from there walk through a part of the *Parroy Forest*, then drive to *Lunéville*.

HOTELS

LUNÉVILLE
GRAND HOTEL DES VOSGES,   Modern comfort.   Garage.
   Telephone 50.

NANCY `
EXCELSIOR HOTEL, GRAND HOTEL D'ANGLETERRE,
   Place Thiers.   Modern comfort.   100 rooms.
   Telephone 4.63.   Restaurant.

HOTEL DE L'EUROPE,   80 rooms.   Modern comfort.
   Angle of the Rue des Carmes and   Electric Lighting.   Central
     Gambetta.   heating.   Bath rooms.
   Telephone 2.06   Garage, 20 cars.

HOTEL TERMINUS,   Modern comfort.   Bath
   In front of the station.   rooms.   Salons.

HOTEL DE L'UNIVERSITÉ ET DU COMMERCE,
   Rue des Carmes.   Bath rooms.   Dark room.
                            Restaurant.   Garage.

SAINT-DIÉ
HOTEL DU GLOBE,   Central heating.   Electric
   Rue Thiers.   Telephone 103.   Lighting.   40 rooms.
                            Garage, 10 cars.

HOTEL DE LA POSTE.   30 rooms.   Garage, 10 cars.

Historical Account

After having been for long an independent province belonging sometimes to a French Prince and sometimes a German one, Lorraine became French for good at the death of her last Duke (1776) Stanislas Leczinski, dethroned King of Poland.

Nancy, chief town of the Lorraine, is the most charming town in the East of France. She owes most of her monuments to the Duke Stanislas. Visit the old town gates, the square Stanislas, the Ducal palace and the Governor's residence. On the Stanislas Square the famous grating is a marvel of the eighteenth century iron-work.

Economical Account

The soil of the Meurthe-and-Moselle is often poor ; in the valleys they produce potatoes and various cereals. For the chief wealth of this region we have to turn to industry. Besides the Briey basin, which will be mentioned in Sector 7, we find numerous ironworks at Frouard, Pompey, Pont-Saint-Vincent, near Nancy.

At Vézelise, Maxeville, Tantonville, they brew notable beers. At Nancy we find quite a variety of industries (shoes, agricultural tools, locksmiths, artistic glass works and furniture). At Dombasle are the big Solway works (chemical products). From different sections of ground they are extracting salt and soda.

Short Account of the Operations

Ph. Rol

Gen. CASTELNAU.

Ph. Rol

Gen. DUBAIL.

The district of Nancy was at the beginning of the war the theatre of a great battle in the open. Lorraine seems to be almost the unique fighting ground. The German effort, resting as it did, mainly on Belgium and on our Northern frontier, resulted in a considerable movement of our defence masses from this zone. A splendid offensive had brought us into the annexed Lorraine as far as Château-Salins and Dieuze. Our storm troops, however, having been reduced in order to meet the requirements of the Northern army, the Germans availed themselves of this opportunity and attacked us violently. Our soldiers were obliged to retreat. There followed the retreat of Morhange. This success made the German Generals over-confident, and the Kaiser dreamed of triumphantly entering Nancy. This dream was effectively destroyed by the extremely skilful manœuvres of Castelnau and Dubail, who knew they could check the enemy on the heights which make up the " Grand Couronne de Nancy."

In vain the Germans attacked our positions of Bayon and Sainte-Geneviève. Though numerically inferior, our soldiers resisted the enemy's onslaughts splendidly. At Sainte-Geneviève 12,000 Prussians attacked one of our regiments which they outnumbered by four to one. They were decimated by the fire of our 75's. They renewed the attack without ceasing. Our artillerymen were short of shells and they mingled with our infantry. The enemy was 600 ft. from our position. Our troops met him with the bayonet and counter-attacked violently. The enemy, surprised, retired and executed no further attack in this region.

Nevertheless, the Germans had progressed to the South and boasted of very soon entering Nancy ; yet they had to retire once again. The Kaiser, arrived there in order to witness the victory of his troops, saw their bloody defeat of September 8, when the supreme German effort was rolled back by the bayonets of our soldiers in the wood of Champenoux.

Sector 4—Nancy

The Germans retired on to the right bank of the Seille, and we established ourselves on the left. From that time the sector was calm and no change of positions on either side took place until the Armistice. There were but few bombardments, only numerous small engagements carried out by groups of bold soldiers. Now and then one of our sections passed the Seille in a canoe, surprised one of the enemy's small posts

Ph. Léon

NANCY—La Place Thiers

and seized some prisoners. Few troops guarded the sector, the posts being far apart and not thick, so that these engagements were relatively easy.

War Facts

NANCY suffered numerous bombardments from long-range guns, and especially from aeroplanes. It was on January 1, 1915, that the first .380 shell burst in the town and about 100 more fell afterwards on the old Lorraine city. But she suffered more particularly from bombs dropped from aeroplanes. The station was peculiarly singled out. On the Square Thiers a ferro-concrete shelter was built to protect the people. The train service never stopped passing Nancy, but embarkation work took place at Jarville.

FROUARD and **POMPEY** are two small industrial towns with a certain number of blast furnaces. The Frouard iron-works ceased working from the beginning of hostilities. Those of Pompey continued uninterruptedly to make rails and shells for our armies, which were in such need of them. That is the reason why the Germans so bitterly concentrated on Pompey both long-range howitzers and aeroplanes.

LE BOIS LE-PRETRE was one of the spots where the trench war was most heavy. There were never any large offensives, but quite a series of local engagements, particularly in 1915 and 1916.

NOMENY.—On August 20, 1914, there was at Nomeny an engagement followed by a three-days' cannonading. The Germans at length occupied the town, and distinguished themselves by nameless atrocities.

" At Nomeny," writes a soldier, " the corpses of the inhabitants lie everywhere, on the staircases, in the cellars, in the street. On a heap of dirt we have found the corpses of two children, and further those of three young girls awfully mutilated. An old man of eighty-six had his hands smashed by a revolver shot in front of his wife's eyes."

FORET-DE-CHAMPENOUX.—It was in the woods of Champenoux before Amance that the German offensive against Nancy was broken.

On September 6, the day of the enemy's furthest advance, Nancy was bombarded by field-guns. On the 8th the Germans attempted a supreme effort in order to take the Lorraine capital. It is said that the Kaiser had come into this region in order to witness the entrance of his troops.

The assault was terrible ; six times the enemy advanced to the attack, but each time he was dispersed by the fire of our 75's. Our victory was complete ; in the evening we passed to the offensive and the enemy was compelled to retire to the banks of the Seille; Nancy remained intact. The region of **MORHANGE, DIEUZE, CHATEAU-SALINES** was conquered by us in August 1914. The forces allocated for this offensive, whose aim it was to block up the communications with Metz, were too weak. Our outflanked troops could not hold out against the enemy's violent shock and the painful retreat of Morhange ensued, which allowed the Germans to pass our frontier and to threaten Nancy.

All this region owes its prosperity to the salt and soda mines, interesting to the visitor.

The **FORET DE PARROY** stretches itself to the north-east of Lunéville; it was the scene of a terrible trench war between two adversaries established at a short distance from each other, and day and night incessant combats took place with grenades and aerial torpedoes; *coups de main* were attempted in order to get hold of a bastion, a hill or a trench. In 1915 and 1916, from Embermenil to Parroy, thousands of mines were exploded, swallowing each time a group of soldiers. Terrible fighting followed for the possession of the tunnel. Once they understood the uselessness of this trench fighting, the sector became a relatively quiet one.

LUNEVILLE.—The Germans prudently entered the town with small patrols on August 22, 1914 ; on the 23rd, they paraded triumphantly. During their stay, numberless exactions were extorted, civilians were killed in the streets by the German sentries, and the suburb of **EINVILLE** was methodically set on fire, the Germans burning it gradually by blocks of three or four houses. They imposed on the small town a fine of 650,000 francs, and every day six hostages taken from among the notables had to remain prisoners of the German Kommandantur. At last, on September 12, after the victory of the Marne, the French dragoons entered the town, which had already been evacuated by the Germans.

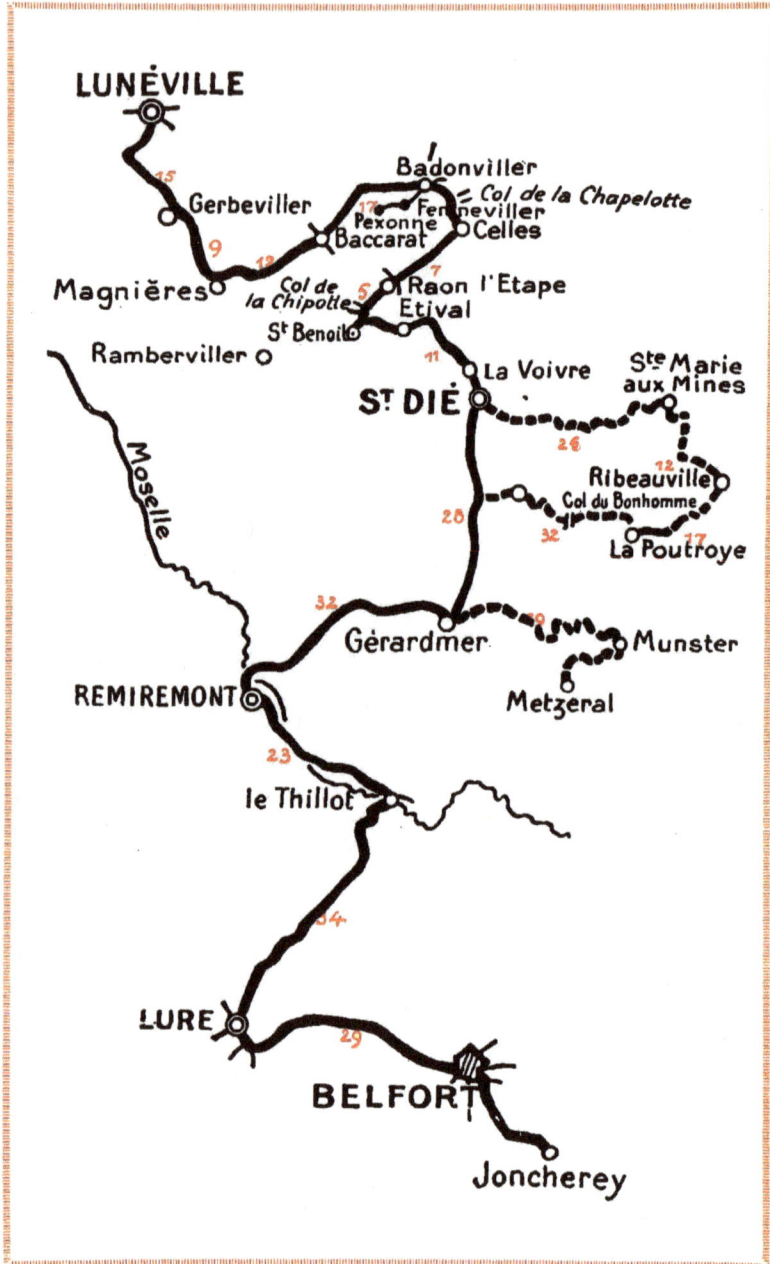

Sector 5—The Vosges

Route

Go out of *Lunéville* through the suburb of *Villers :* proceed to *Gerbeviller* through *Xermamenil :* stop at Gerbeviller.

Leaving Gerbeviller take the road of *Magnières*.

At Magnières, turn to the left and drive on to *Baccarat*. At the northern entrance of Baccarat, take the road of *Merviller :* leave this village and at *Montigny* turn to the right. Go on to *Badonviller* and visit Badonviller.

If you have time, take the road of *Pexonne*, visit *Fenneviller* and Pexonne, and return to Badonviller, there take the road of *Celles*, a very picturesque one, almost following the lines ; one may see on the left the hill of *Chapelotte*. From Celles go down to *Raon-l'Etape*. Visit it and, on issuing, take the road of *Ramberviller :* at the first crossing, visit the tombs of the *Col de la Chipotte*. Drive to *Saint-Benoît* and come back to the crossing of *La Chipotte ;* there turn to the right.

After having passed *Etival*, you reach the big road of Saint-Dié ; stop at *La Voivre*, then drive on to *Saint-Dié*.

From Saint-Dié push on to *Gérardmer*, or, from Saint-Dié go to *Sainte-Marie-aux-Mines ;* at Sainte-Marie-aux-Mines turn to the right and go down to *Ribeauville :* from here reach *La Poutroye* and then cross the old frontier at the hill *Bonhomme*, reach *Fraize*, then go to *Gérardmer*.

From Gérardmer you may go to *Munster*, and from Munster to *Metzeral*, but in this last section the route is very difficult.

Or you may reach *Remiremont* directly from Gérardmer.

Going out from Remiremont take the route of Mulhouse to *le Thillot*, there turn to the right, visit *Lure*, and from Lure push to *Belfort*. From Belfort you may go on to *Joncherey*.

87

||||||||||||||||||||||||||||||||||||||||||||||||||||||||||||||||||||||||||||||||||||||||||||||||||||||||||

HOTELS

BELFORT

GRAND HOTEL DU TONNEAU D'OR.
Boulevard Carnot. Modern comfort.
Telephone 226. Garage.

HOTEL DE L'ANCIENNE POSTE. Recommended by T.C.F. and
Place Corbus. A.C.F. Modern comfort.
Telephone 2.35. Garage.

HOTEL DE LA VICTOIRE AND RESTAURANT JEANNIN.
Place d'Armes. First-class restaurant.

EPINAL

GRAND HOTEL DU LOUVRE ET D'ANGLETERRE AND
HOTEL SUISSE REUNIS. 100 rooms. Modern comfort.
Garage 20 cars. All languages spoken.

VESOUL

GRAND HOTEL DE L'EUROPE. 50 rooms. Bathrooms.
Garage.

Historical Account

The department of the Vosges belonged to the province of Lorraine, and shared her fate until it was made a department at the Revolution. In 1814, the inhabitants of the Vosges rose against the invader, and led a terrible guerilla war against the Prussian and Russian troops. A century later there was a new invasion. This time it was of short duration, and only a few weak parts of the department remained occupied by the Germans after October 1914.

Economic Account

The region of the Vosges is prosperous both through its agriculture and its industry. Various cereals are produced, and the rich valleys breed cattle. The metallurgical trades (locksmiths, cast iron, lathes) and the textile industry (linen, cloth, cotton, lace) are prosperous. There are numerous paper factories and works for making printed fabrics. Adequate mineral resources assist the prosperity of this region (Bussang, Contrexéville, Plombières, Saint-Vallier, Vittel).

Short Account of the Operations

Ph. Pirou

Gen. MAUD'HUY

The region of the Vosges was from the beginning the scene of obstinate fighting. From August 8, 1914, our troops penetrated into Alsace, and succeeded in getting hold of Sainte-Marie-aux-Mines and of a series of hills which up to that time had delineated the frontier. The necessity of defence against a Northern invasion having considerably drawn upon our forces in the East, and our troops having felt the repercussion of the Morhange retreat since August 21, we had to retire. The Germans broke into our territory as far as Raon-l'Etape and Saint-Dié. We succeeded in checking them at the hill of La Chipotte, and after the splendid Marne victory our enthusiastic troops repelled the enemy to the other side of the Alsace frontier. From that moment the Vosges remained a calm sector, a true sector of repose.

The lines were far from each other, and the conformation of the ground rendered an advance difficult for both sides. Nevertheless, there were a few bad corners, as for instance the hill of Chapelotte, where bombardments and local engagements were frequent. Each adversary sought to capture a few prisoners in order to get from them information concerning the political and military situation of the enemy. Even if no heavy fighting took place, yet the situation of our soldiers was not less painful, on account of the difficult roads to the mountains covered with snow for the whole winter.

War Facts

GERBEVILLER.—Gerbeviller offers the tourist one of the most fearful pictures of ruin and desolation one could meet on the front. Before the war a small town full of life and gaiety, it had to suffer very much from German barbarism ; it was not the shells which reduced her to such a state of ruins, but deliberate fires produced by the German soldiers by means of sulphur sticks and inflammable powder pastilles, of which samples have been found in the haversacks of the German infantrymen. The people had to suffer a great deal from the Teutonic brutality, as women and children were killed in the streets. On one occasion fifteen old men with white hair were shot in groups of five. A German officer, seated at a table, while drinking, gave the signal of execution by carrying the glass to his lips. More than forty inhabitants perished through fire or bullets.

89

Against the German's brutal thirst for blood and horror, we are able to set the example of charity and grandeur of soul shown at that time by the Sisters of Charity of Gerbeviller, under the direction of Sister Julia. A simple country girl, she knew how to find in her faith and love enough strength of will to resist the Germans who wanted to force their way to the asylum door, where she kept several wounded French soldiers. For more than three weeks she nursed German wounded. When people speak to her of what she has done, she quite simply replies, " But there is nothing extraordinary in it." A sublime virtue, which has been rewarded by the cross of the Légion d'Honneur.

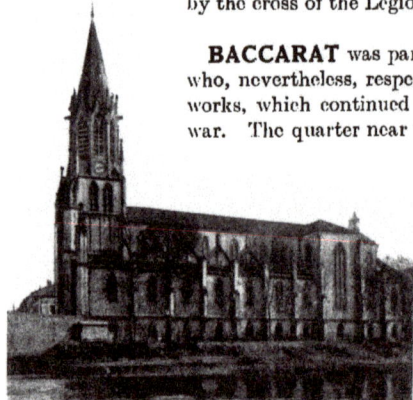

BACCARAT was partly burnt by the Germans, who, nevertheless, respected the famous cut-glass works, which continued working during the whole war. The quarter near the church was set on fire by order of the German military authorities. The tower of the church has been partially destroyed by shells.

BADONVILLER. Badonviller was occupied three times by the Germans. Twenty-three civilians perished during these various inroads. The Mayor's wife was shot in the sight of her

Ph. Léon

BACCARAT. The Church

husband in the street ; a woman with a baby in her arms and an old man of 78 fell a little further on under the German bullets. The fighting lines passed at about 1,500 ft. from Badonviller, and the shells bursting in the cemetery (behind the church) reopened the tombs and stripped the corpses to the skin. The church was used as target by the enemy's artillery during almost the whole war, and until the arrival of the Americans in this sector (July, 1918) a certain number of inhabitants remained in Badonviller in spite of the proximity to the line of fire.

FENNEVILLER was burnt in August, 1914. Only a few ruins remain.

PEXONNE, on the contrary, remained untouched until July, 1918. At that time the Americans caused the little village to be evacuated ; they made several attacks in the sector. The Germans riposted by bombarding Pexonne, and within a few weeks reduced it to its present condition.

Sector 5—The Vosges

SAINTE-MARIE-AUX-MINES owes her name to ancient copper and zinc mines. It was taken by our Alpine Chasseurs on August 8, 1914. It was lost on August 21, after the affair of Morhange, and reconquered by our troops after our victory of the Marne and our return offensive in the Vosges.

RAON-L'ETAPE is a pretty little town of 4,500 inhabitants. It was occupied for a few days by the Germans at the end of August, 1914. There, too, they behaved like vandals, setting on fire the private houses, exacting hostages and war fines.

COL DE LA CHIPOTTE was a terrible spot called by both adversaries "the hole of death." There was a succession of twelve to thirteen days' fighting there, principally with bayonets, knives and rifle butts. Numerous French and German tombs stand amidst the big Vosges pines and cover all the neighbouring hills.

SAINT BENOIT, near Raon l'Etape, has suffered almost the same fate as Gerbeviller, the village having been entirely burnt down by the German hordes.

LA VOIVRE was the witness of an instance of German barbarism which well denotes the warped mind of our enemies. The Parish Priest is accused of espionage for having in his house a map on which small flags marking the enemy's lines were fixed. The troopers get hold of him, and, while they take him away, they announce that he will be shot. The small group is met on the way by an old woman who puts in a word for him to the sergeant. She is apprehended, and the same fate is promised to her. Further, an old man, seeing the two condemned, beseeches the sergeant, but he is apprehended also. All three are taken out of the village and put against a wall, the Priest standing and extending over the two old people his pardon. The firing squad fires suddenly, but only the Priest, pierced with bullets, falls, the two old people having been spared by order.

SAINT-DIE.—25,000 inhabitants. At the intersection of the great Transvosgian roads, Saint Dié is divided into three parts ; the colonial town, surrounding the Cathedral (which goes back as far as the seventh century), the old town on the right bank of the Meurthe, and the suburb on the left bank.

See there the Cathedral (choir and transept of the thirteenth century) and Notre-Dame Church (eleventh century), joined by a cloister. There are spinning factories, cotton houses and smelting furnaces.

Saint Dié was occupied by the Germans when they advanced on August 22, 1914, after their victory in the region of Morhange. There also the Germans behaved with their habitual contempt for the people's rights. They massacred, in particular, thirty French soldiers who, having no ammunition, had given themselves up.

91

Sector 5—The Vosges

METZERAL was taken by us from June 15 to 22, 1915, by an infantry battalion and several battalions of Chasseurs Alpins. On June 15, after a scientific artillery preparation, the first attack was delivered.

The Chasseurs' band was playing "Sidi Brahim," and that of the infantry the "Marseillaise." The fight was particularly heavy in the town of Metzeral; the factory of Steinsbruck was taken on the 17th and 21st. They outflanked Metzeral by the north, and our Alpini reached the station. The Germans had to evacuate the little town, after having burnt down all the houses.

BELFORT, 20,000 inhabitants, comprises three parts: the old town on the right banks of the Savoureuse (church of Saint-Denis), the fortress and the citadel (the lion of Bartholdi cut in the granite), and, finally, the new town on the left bank of the river. In 1870, Colonel Denfert-Rochereau, with 16,000 men, sustained a siege of three months and a half against 30,000 Germans and surrendered only by order of the Government on February 18, 1871, the very day of the armistice. Owing to his heroic defence, the town of Belfort was allowed to remain French.

Belfort is a commercial town (wine, wood, iron) and an industrial one (spinning and textile). The immigration of the Alsatians in 1870 helped the economic development of Belfort considerably.

JONCHEREY, near Delle, on the Swiss border, was the witness of the first engagement which cost human lives on both sides. On August 2, 1914, at the time when war was not yet declared, Lieutenant Mayer, of the 5th German Hunters, followed by a patrol of six or seven cavalrymen, broke into French soil. The reconnaissance arrived before a French post established on the Belfort road. As a kind of answer to the words "Who goes there?" of the Corporal Peugeot, Mayer fired three revolver shots at him; the corporal fell mortally wounded, the first victim of the war; and the lieutenant was shot instantly by one of Peugeot's comrades.

See in the cemetery both tombs, that of Corporal Peugeot and the German lieutenant.

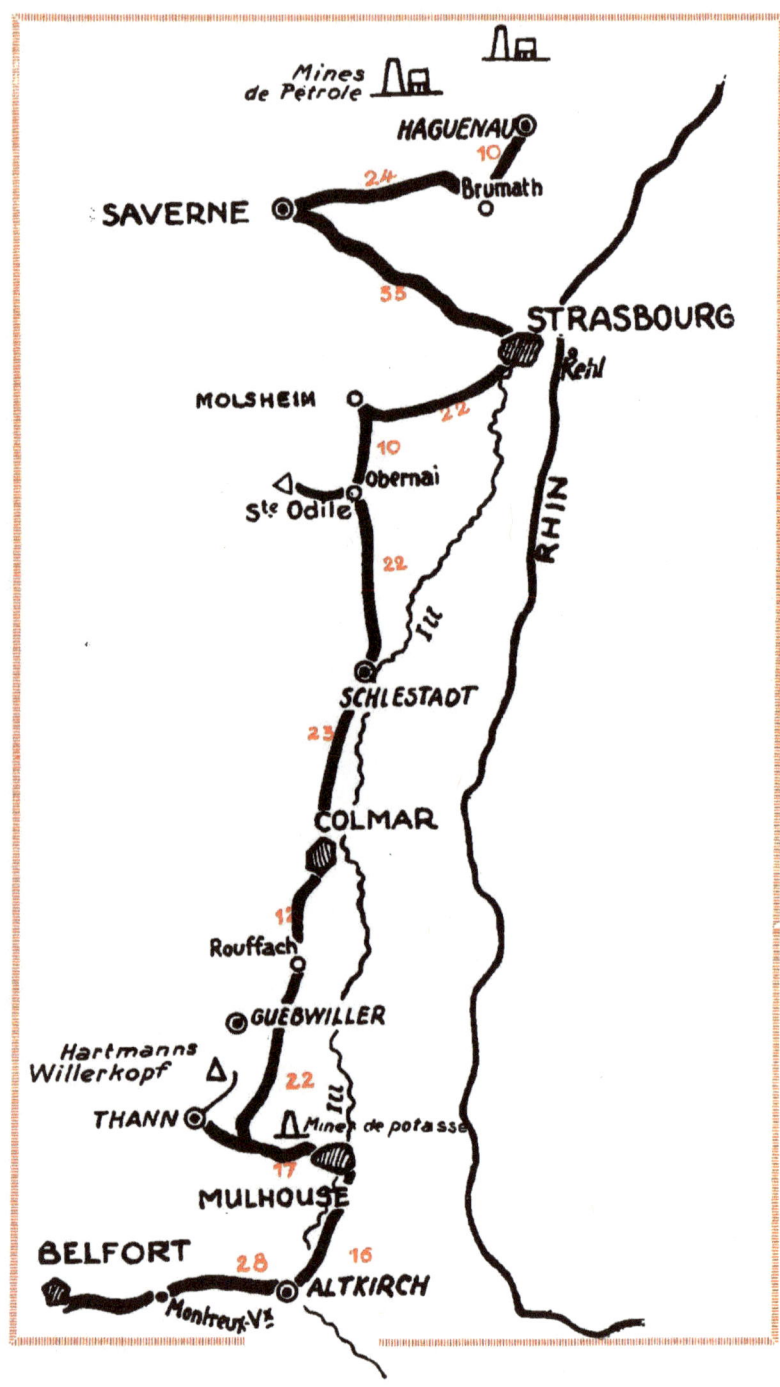

Sector 6—Alsace

Route

The tourist will leave *Belfort*, cross the ancient frontier at *Montreux-Vieux*, visit *Altkirch*, *Mulhouse*, the potash mines, *Thann :* from there he will visit *Hartmannswillerkopf*. Then he will take the main road of *Colmar* through *Rouffach :* a little detour to the left will allow him before Rouffach to visit *Guebwiller*.

After visiting Colmar, reach *Schlestadt* and *Obernai :* from there a trip to *Sainte-Odile* ; from Obernai go up again to *Molsheim*, there turn to the right and reach *Strasbourg*.

After the visit to Strasbourg and *Kehl*, go to *Saverne* by the direct route, then from Saverne reach *Haguenau* through *Brumath*, visit the oil-fields northward of Haguenau.   See map Page 101.

HOTELS

COLMAR

HOTEL TERMINUS.	Modern comfort. 50 rooms. Garage.
HOTEL NATIONALE. Rue de la Gare.	Modern comfort. 30 rooms. Garage.
HOTEL DE L'AGNEAU NOIR. 12 and 14 Avenue de la République. Telephone 101.	

HAGUENAU

HOTEL DU RAISIN. 37 Grande Rue.	Modern comfort. 30 rooms. Garage 10.

MULHOUSE

HOTEL CENTRAL. 14 Rue du Sauvage.	Modern comfort. 100 rooms. Garage 30.
GRAND HOTEL NATIONAL. Rue du Sauvage. Passage Central. Telephone 228.	Modern comfort. 100 rooms.
HOTEL DE L'EUROPE. 11 Avenue du Commerce.	Electric Lighting. Central heating. Baths.

SAVERNE

HOTEL DE LA GARE. Near the Station.	Modern Comfort. Garage.

SCHLESTADT

HOTEL NANSER. In front of the Station.	Garage 10. Modern comfort.

STRASBOURG

GRAND HOTEL DE LA VILLE DE PARIS.
Place Broglié. Centre.　　　Modern comfort.
　Telephone 64.　　　　　　Garage 40.

PALACE HOTEL, MAISON ROUGE.
Place Kleber.　　　　　　　Modern comfort.　Famous
　Telephone 122.　　　　　　kitchen and cellar.　Music at
　　　　　　　　　　　　　　　table d'hôte.

HOTEL NATIONAL.　　　　　Modern comfort.　Baths and
　In front of the Station.　　　shower.　120 rooms.
　　　　　　　　　　　　　　　Garage 30.

HOTEL CHRISTOPHE.　　　　Modern comfort.
　In front of Station.　　　　Garage.
　Telephone 380.

HOTEL CONTINENTAL.　　　　70 rooms.　Garage.
　On the old wine market.　　Modern comforts.

Historical Account

Alsace was incorporated with France towards the end of the seventeenth century. At the time of the Revolution, she seized warmly the cause of liberty, and in an enthusiastic joy she declared of her own free will to be an integral part of the French nation. It was in Strasbourg, in Marie Diétrich's house, that Rouget de l'Isle sang for the first time our " Marseillaise " (1792).

In 1870, Alsace was abandoned after the battles of Froeschwiller (Woerth) and Forbach (Spichern). On May 10, 1871, for the last time the Alsatians acted as French electors, and chose representatives who protested warmly against Alsace's annexation. From 1870 until 1914, this province resisted all attempts at Germanisation and remained inherently French. It was amidst an indescribable joy that the Alsatians welcomed our victorious troops at the end of November 1918, when they brought back to their dear country the tricolor.

Economic Account

Alsace stretches between the Vosges and the Rhine, from the Swiss frontier to the North of the Haguenau Woods. It comprises two perfectly distinct parts : the mountains covered with woods, and the plain lining the left bank of the Rhine. Alsace's plain is particularly fertile, and was for ages coveted by the Germans established on the opposite bank of the river. They cultivate corn, flax, and malt. On the first range of Vosges Hills are numerous vineyards producing a famous wine, but the present wealth of Alsace consists in her oil-fields and potash mines.

Short Account of the Operations

Ph. Rol

Gen. PAU

The southern part of Alsace was the scene of our first successes. They were more dramatic than lasting. After the incursion of the German patrol on August 2, 1914, which brought the deaths of the first French and the first German at Joncherey, our troops moved forward and General D'Amade occupied Altkirch. The soldiers were received everywhere with a delirious enthusiasm, but continued their march and the next day Mulhouse was covering them with flowers. But we were not organised. The enemy attacked us with superior numbers, and we had to evacuate the town.

It was then that General Pau organised a clever manœuvre, and on August 19 forced the Germans after heavy fighting to abandon Mulhouse a second time. The unhappy course of events in Belgium and Lorraine compelled the High Command to restrict the army sectors in Alsace, and so we had to give up the offensive and even abandon Mulhouse and Altkirch. We succeeded in keeping Thann and Dannemarie. The Alsace sector has been during the whole war relatively a calm one, except at one point, the Hartmannswillerkopf, where heavy engagements were frequently in progress. At the time when Germany cried for mercy, a large offensive was being prepared and our Eastern army could have conquered in one bound the old Alsace territory.

We entered this hereditary French soil as conquerors. The Alsatians welcomed our troops with an extraordinary enthusiasm. Their cheers were a more conclusive and moving plebiscite than all the voting papers one could have gathered.

In the large towns there took place impressive parades ; our army commanders had the honour to enter Strasbourg, Colmar, and Mulhouse at the head of their troops. But in the small towns and villages, the welcome, though not so solemn, was no less enthusiastic. Our soldiers were covered with flowers, kissed and spoilt by everybody. Our young soldiers and the girls danced gaily throughout the night, whilst the wisest talked with the old Alsatians over good brown beer.

G

War Facts

ALTKIRCH is a small town of 5,000 inhabitants (textile, corn, breweries). On August 7, 1914, a French infantry brigade occupied the trenches where the Germans had only been able to organise a feeble resistance ; they entered the town amidst the immense joy of the inhabitants. Frontier signposts were torn out of the ground and carried in triumph through the beflagged streets, and heaps of flowers were thrown at our victorious troops.

MULHOUSE is the largest town of Southern Alsace. It is a prosperous city with 120,000 inhabitants, where industry has been greatly developed (spinning mills, dye works, mechanical constructions). At its own request it was united with France in 1798.

On August 8, 1914, the French, without difficulty, entered Mulhouse, and there were the same foolish manifestations of joy and enthusiasm as on the day before at Altkirch ; we were not in numbers, however, and on the 10th we had to evacuate Mulhouse before the attack of two German army corps. The enemy, furious at the reception the Alsatians had given our troops, put in prison the most Francophile of the inhabitants, young and old. On August 14, a strong French army attacked again, and penetrated into Mulhouse. Shortly afterwards we suffered heavy losses in the region of Morhange, and we had to evacuate Mulhouse a second time. When, after the armistice, our victorious troops entered Mulhouse it was a frenzy of joy.

The **POTASH MINES.**—North of Mulhouse, in the triangle formed by Mulhouse, Cernay and Ensisheims, are numerous wells for the extraction of potash and important beds extending over all this region to depths varying from 1,500 to 2,400 ft. The potash, whose importance is known as a fertiliser and raw material for the chemical industry, is a source of incalculable prosperity for this district. Certain people estimate these potash beds to contain about 100 milliards. They were discovered quite accidentally ; an old lady who never dreamt of wealth owned a few acres of ground ; one of her friends, an engineer, exploited the grounds, and believed he had found some coal. After two fruitless attempts, which absorbed all his capital and the owner's income, he discovered, when at the end of his resources and patience, a strange mineral, partly white and partly grey, with fine sparkling crystals ; it was the potash salt, the dream of avarice. Soon after, these beds were properly sounded.

Up to that time Germany, with the beds of Stassfurt in Saxony, possessed the monopoly for the selling of potash to the whole of Europe. The German Government, annoyed at seeing competition arise in Alsace, limited, by two arbitrary decrees, the conditions under which the potash could be extracted. The exploitation, having become free, will produce from now an enormous quantity of that mineral, which will contribute to the improvement of the Alsatian and French agriculture. Note that the sylvinite (potash mineral) of Alsace is much richer in pure potash than the sylvinite of Saxony. Quite a series of wells is in existence three miles to the north of Mulhouse (mine Anna), another series is situated about 5 miles north-west on the other side of Lutter-bach on the line Mulhouse-Cernay (mine Else, mine Joseph).

La Science et la Vie.

POTASH MINES

THANN.—It is a small town of 9,000 inhabitants, an industrial and commercial town, mainly occupied with spinning mills, mechanical construction works, and wine trade. This little town remained French during the whole war, and M. Poincaré delivered here the greeting of France to reconquered Alsace. Thann contains a nice Gothic church, of about the fourteenth or fifteenth century.

HARTMANNSWILLERKOPF, which our soldiers nicknamed the "old Armand," was the scene of heavy fighting during the years 1915 and 1916. The ridge was taken and retaken several times. Our Alpin Chasseurs distinguished themselves in this sector. It was incessant fighting with grenades, mines, aerial torpedoes, and destructive fighting, more terrible perhaps than a regular attack. The soldier was feeling uninterruptedly the menace of a bombardment, of a coup-de-main, of a gas attack or a bayonet charge. He had always to be on the watch, even when he himself was not ordered to the assault. A thousand instances of individual heroism could illustrate the combats of " the old Armand."

COLMAR is the capital of the Upper-Rhine district, of about 38,000 inhabitants, trading with wines, beer, skins and clothes. Visit the Church of Saint-Martin, the Kaufhaus, which exists since the fifteenth century, and a few old houses. Our soldiers received an enthusiastic welcome at Colmar.

General Castelnau entered the town in state on November 22, 1918.

SCHLESTADT.—It is at Schlestadt that stands the old castle of Hoh-Koenigsbourg, one of the oldest monuments of Alsatian history (twelfth century). It was rebuilt very badly by William II, who sometimes stayed there in order to affirm his domination over Alsace, this castle having served once as a residence to the Counts of Alsace.

SAINTE-ODILE.—At Hohembourg ; north-west of Obernai stands on a hill the monastery of Sainte-Odile, a shrine dear to all the Alsatians. The hill and the environs are most picturesque, and from the monastery's terrace one sees the whole plain of Alsace extending to the sun, its rich meadows, its wheat fields and hop gardens, from whence the red-roofed villages emerge. Half-way up the hill there is an old wall built once by the Gauls against the invasions of the Germans.

STRASBOURG (180,000 inhabitants) became French in 1681 and shared France's destiny until 1870. On August 13, 1870, it was besieged by the German troops, and a fearful bombardment destroyed many houses, the theatre, the library and the new temple ; it had to surrender on September 27.

Strasbourg comprises an old and a new town. The old, French, very picturesque town stands on the banks of the Ill. The cathedral is a marvel, a masterpiece of Gothic art. The Hotel du Commerce (ancient Mayoral building) and quite a number of Alsatian houses of the Middle Ages, or more recent, but all quite original, are admired. Between the Ill and the Rhine stands the modern town built by the Germans. The Hotel de la Poste (Post Office) and Kaiser William's Palace are typical examples of their bad taste.

SAVERNE.—9,000 inhabitants. On the borders of Alsace and Lorraine, an old town known already at the time of the Roman occupation under the name of Tres Tabernae, " the three taverns." The town has prosperous mechanical industries, breweries and, in the neighbourhood of the town, clay quarries in full working order.

Saverne was famous in 1913 owing to the exploits of Lieut. Von Forstner. His practical jokes on the Alsatian soldiers engendered a slight revolt amongst the inhabitants who had remained

French. It was an opportunity for the Kaiser to edict Draconian measures with regard to the Alsatians, but it was, nevertheless, a splendid manifestation of the patriotism of the Alsatians.

The **OIL-FIELDS.**—At the North of Strasbourg, at about 20 miles between the Forest of Haguenau and Wissembourg, there are oil-fields

La Science et la Vie.

OIL-FIELDS

called the Mines of Pechelbronn. These mines in reality are near Biblisheim on the Wissembourg line and North of the Nield-Wald woods. The extraction attained 33,500 tons ; it is little compared with the Caucasus or American oil-fields, but considering the actual price of mineral oils, it is no less a source of wealth for Alsace. This oil makes excellent petrol.

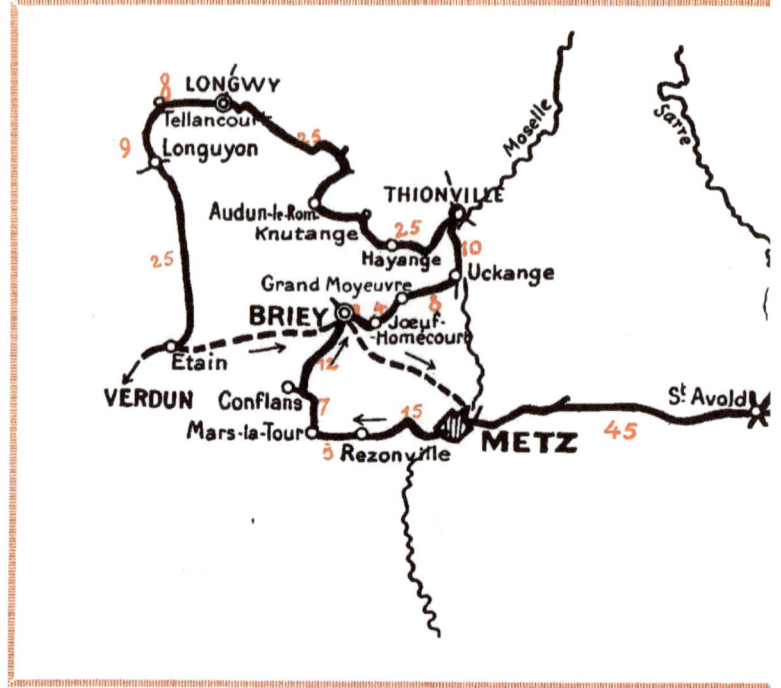

Sector 7—Lorraine

Route

The tourist leaves *Haguenau*, end of Sector 6, and manages to visit the battlefield of *Reichshoffen*, famous since 1870. At Reichshoffen turn to the right and pass to *Woerth*, then to *Soultz*, then turn to the left ; visit *Wissembourg*, then *Landau*. At the entrance of Landau take the road of *Deux-Ponts* ; descend again south of *Bitche*, visit this little town, then take the road of *Sarreguemines :* from Sarreguemines go to *Sarrebruck*. Then go down to *Saint-Avold*, on the way visit *Forbach*. From Saint-Avold reach *Metz*. From Metz reach *Conflans*, taking the route of *Rezonville* and turning to the right at *Mars-la-Tour*. From Conflans reach *Briey*. From Briey go to *Jœuf-Homécourt*, where you will visit the naval works. Cross the ancient frontier, and pass to *Grand Moyeuvre*. At *Uckange* turn to the left and reach *Thionville*. Visit Thionville. From there go to *Audun-le-Roman*, passing through the big industrial centres of, *Hayange* and *Knutange*. From Audun-le-Roman go to *Longwy*, returning by the main road of Metz-Longwy to *Aumetz*. From Longwy reach *Longuyon*, through *Tellancourt :* from Longuyon, *Etain*, and from Etain, *Metz* or *Verdun*.

Sector 7—Lorraine

HOTELS

METZ

GRAND HOTEL
(formerly Hotel de l'Europe).
4 Rue des Clercs.

100 rooms. Modern
comfort. Garage 30.

HOTEL ROYAL
(near the station).

Modern comfort. Lift.
90 rooms. Garage.

HOTEL CENTRAL.
Near the Station.
Telephone 570.

Modern comfort. Electric
Lighting. Central heating.
Garage.

HOTEL NATIONAL ET GRANDE BRASSERIE.
In front of the Station.

Modern comfort.

SARREBOURG

HOTEL DU LION D'OR.
Centre of the town.
Rue de la Marne.

Comfortable rooms.
Famous kitchen.
Garage.

THIONVILLE

HOTEL TERMINUS.
Near the Station.

Modern comfort.
Garage.

Historical Account

Lorraine was for some time an independent province. It became, in the eighteenth century, the property of Stanislas Leczinski, then King of Poland. It knew under his rule a most prosperous epoch. At his death (1766) it became French. In 1790 it formed the Departments of Meuse, Vosges, Moselle and Meurthe. The treaty of Frankfort in 1871 deprived us of a part of Lorraine. The annexed Lorraine, with Metz for its capital, remained truly French and very much attached to its traditions. The Germans succeeded no better in making the Lorraines forget their nationality than the Alsatians. It was with a touching piety that during the whole term of the German occupation the inhabitants celebrated the anniversary of the battles of 1870, which had been fought on the Lorraine soil.

Economic Account

The annexed Lorraine is a very rich and industrial region owing to the numerous iron mines and the proximity of the Sarre coal. Hayange, Moyeuvre and Knutange, are large industrial centres.

An important salt bed extends under the whole country, limited on the frontier of 1871 only by Bismarck's will. The works of Chateau-Salins, Dieuze and Sarralbe and of other less important places produce 190,000 tons of salt and soda. These mines belong largely to the Solway Company, and to owners in Alsace and Lorraine.

||||||||||||||||||||||||||||||||||||||||||||||||||||||||||||||||||||||||||||||||||||||||||||||||||||||||||||||||||||||||||||||||||

General Considerations

We have introduced the Lorraine and the Basin of Briey into our routes, though no fighting took place there, but everybody will, no doubt, wish to go through our old province torn away from her mother by Germany against all principles of right and justice.

As regards the Briey basin, it will be interesting to visit the large metallurgical centre which, joining the centres of annexed Lorraine, forms in the east of France the most important industrial group in the world for the extraction of iron and its transformation into steel.

REICHSHOFFEN is the scene of the eighteenth-century combat, which was, perhaps, more widely celebrated than any other. Actually there has been no battle at Reichshoffen ; the famous cavalry charge was but an episode of the battle of Froeschwiller. The Germans had succeeded in getting a foot on the plateau of Morsbroom ; to drive them out, two cuirassier regiments (General Michel's brigade) were launched on the enemy. On their cuirasses the shots resounded like hail on windows on a stormy day. They rush into the village of Morsbroom, but their impetus breaks against the barricades hastily raised in the streets. It was a veritable march of death. Two-thirds of the brigade fell in order to save the honour of the French army.

WISSEMBOURG.—8,000 inhabitants. See the church of the thirteenth century and the ruins of a Benedictine abbey of the seventh century. It was at Wissembourg that one of the first battles of the 1870 war was delivered. Five thousand men of Abel Douays division were obliterated by 40,000 of the German Crown Prince's.

LANDAU.—10,000 inhabitants. Gothic church of the thirteenth century. Active wine and foreign goods trade. Furniture and cloth manufactories.

BITCHE is a very old fortress, famous for the splendid resistance it offered in 1870. Encircled on August 8, it resisted during the whole war the enemy's assaults. It was defended by 3,000 heroes under Lieut.-Col. Teyssier until two months after the preliminaries of peace were signed, when the little fortress opened her gates on March 24, 1871. The garrison left the place with the flags flying, arms and baggage retained.

SARREGUEMINES has a population of nearly 20,000 inhabitants. It is an important centre for the velvet industry, and, in addition, 3,000 workmen are employed in a chinaware factory.

SARREBRUCK is the centre of the important coal basin of the Sarre (20,000 inhabitants). It was at Sarrebruck that the first engagement of the 1870 war was delivered. Here the Imperial French Prince received his baptism of fire.

THE SARRE BASIN.—France is suffering principally from lack of coal. The possession of the Sarre basin will be of great value for our national industry. The coal basin extends over an area of 155,000 hectares, from Frankelhotz in the Palatinate to Karlingen in Lorraine. The total extraction is 17 million tons, and 3 million more than the quantity of coal we had to purchase abroad before the war. The Lorraine iron industry absorbs 11 million, so that there are 6 millions left for the remainder of the country. Even with the Sarre Basin we are not rich in coal, yet we shall be less poor.

FORBACH remains for ever famous by the battle of August 5, 1870, begun by the German army of Steinmetz. The 30,000 men of General Froissart fought desperately until night against an enemy superior in numbers. Finally, they had to retreat, abandon their ground, and retire to Metz.

METZ, 60,000 inhabitants, has a splendid cathedral commenced in 1332, with a beautiful nave enhanced by admirable stained glass windows. In 1552 Charles V ceded the town to France. Since then it remained impregnable, and was named Metz-la-Pucelle. In 1870 General Bazaine, with the whole Lorraine army, allowed himself to be encircled in this town after heavy battles at Borny, Gravelotte, and Saint-Privat (August 14, 1870). He capitulated on October 27, delivering without a shot 170,000 men, 6,000 officers, amongst whom were three marshals of France, and fifty-two flags which could not be burnt by their regiments.

GRAVELOTTE-MARS-LA-TOUR, REZONVILLE, well-known battlefields of the 1870 war. On August 16 we had almost won a victory, but during the night Bazaine retired to Saint-Privat, and on the 17th his army was surrounded and had to take shelter in Metz.

The Basin of **BRIEY**—Since the violent polemics which have taken place around the Briey question, everybody in France knows our ferruginous basin north of the Meurthe-et-Moselle. One could have asked oneself why, in 1871, the Germans left us such a prize. To tell the truth, they did not know it themselves. People were then exploiting in the Briey region an iron mineral, highly phosphorescent and called the " Minette Lorraine " ; but, owing to the phosphor, the utilisation of this mineral was very difficult and expensive, so that the produce of the Lorraine mines was a minimum one when, in 1871, they traced the French frontier. Doubtless Bismarck would have kept the whole basin of Briey had he been able to foresee the future. Since that time they have found means to treat this phosphorescent mineral ; with the " bessemer " process one obtains excellent steel from the Lorraine mines, and the slags resulting from dephosphorisation make very good fertilisers. Since this discovery the exploitation of the mines has naturally increased, to the vexation of the Germans, among whose aims of war the taking of the Briey basin was an avowed one.

The Lorraine basin stretched on the right and left of the 1871 frontier, on the right there was the Metz basin, on the left that of Nancy, Briey, and Longwy. From now on, these two basins are adjacent, and

Sector 7—Lorraine

consequently the 21 million tons of mineral from the basin, added to the 18 million of the Briey basin, make a total production of 39 millions for our Lorraine, while Germany, if she holds the Silesian mines, will only have 4 million tons. So France, with her total production of 41 million tons (2 millions from the Saint-Etienne and Normandy mines), ranks second among the world iron-producing powers, after the United States (55 millions), and long before England (15 millions).

Before the war, this mineral was exploited on the spot with coal and coke from the German coal mines. But the Sarre basin is now ours, and an important industrial trust has been formed in the North of Lorraine, a group which, through its enormous output of iron, may become the most important metallurgical centre of the whole world.

The principal zones of the French exploitation were Longwy, Jœuf-Homécourt and Briey. With our victory we become the owners of the mines of Ottange, Hayange, Moyeuvre and Knutange.

THIONVILLE.—10,000 inhabitants; a fortress on the Moselle. The Germans captured it in 1870 after fourteen days' furious bombardment; wood, wine, cattle, tobacco trade.

LONGWY.—8,000 inhabitants; industrial centre amidst the iron mines. Longwy makes steels out of the cast iron of her blast furnaces. For many years it was a fortress, and in 1871 it surrendered only after two months of fierce siege. Obsolete for twenty years, she could, nevertheless, arrest her enemy for eight days under her walls in 1914.

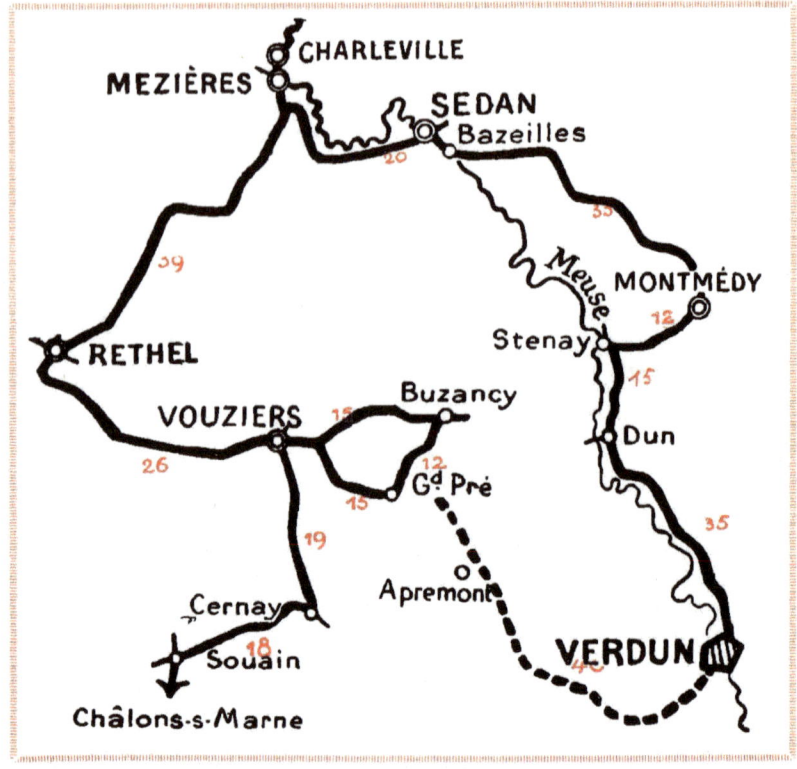

Sector 8—The Ardennes
Route

Start from *Verdun*. Follow the Meuse through *Dun* and *Stenay*. At Stenay turn to the right and visit *Montmédy*.

From Montmédy reach *Sedan*, 500 metres before Sedan pass to *Bazeilles*. Visit Sedan, then cross the Meuse and reach *Mézières-Charleville*. From Mézières-Charleville go down to Rethel.

From Rethel, reach *Vouziers*, then *Buzancy*, on the route of *Montmédy*. At Buzancy turn to the right and reach *Grand-Pré*. From Grand-Pré regain Vouziers, and from Vouziers, *Chalons-sur-Marne* through *Cernay* and *Souain* : or go down to Apremont and Verdun, following the Meuse.

If the tourist wishes to visit all the sectors, he should take the following route : Verdun, Grand-Pré, Buzancy, Vouziers, Rethel, Mézières, Maubeuge, and from the last-named he will take the route of Sector 9 in the reverse direction.

108

HOTELS

CHARLEVILLE
GRAND HOTEL DU LION D'ARGENT.
  20 Rue Thiers.   Modern comfort.
                                    Big garage.

HOTEL DU NORD.   Modern comfort.
  In front of station and the Square. Garage.

From 1914 to 1916 the Hotel kitchen was used to prepare the Kaiser's meals. He lived at the Villa Corneau, near the Hotel. In order to establish communication between the two buildings a passage was opened in the wall of the garden. A banquet was arranged on January 27, 1915, by the Kaiser, in the big hall of the hotel, for the Staff officers.

MAUBEUGE
HOTEL DE LA POSTE ET DU NORD.
                                 Garage.

SEDAN
HOTEL DE METZ.   Good Kitchen.
  Alsace-Lorraine Square.   Garage.

Historical Account

The Ardennes region, previously a part of the Champagne Province, early became French territory. Sedan has remained gloomily famous through the capitulation here of the Chalons army, commanded by MacMahon, on September 2, 1870. After the heavy battles of Beaumont and Bazeilles the last French regular army was encircled in Sedan. The Emperor Napoleon III, thinking the town was unable to defend itself, ordered the white flag to be displayed, and surrendered with the whole army (120,000 men), a bombardment of only a few hours having killed and wounded 17,000 men.

Economic Account

The Ardennes are composed of vast plateaux covered with forests with numerous marshes at their feet. It would have been industrially a very poor region if large improvements had not been introduced in the nineteenth century. They now produce cereals and a little wine. They extract from her soil coal, iron, sand, slates (Fumay) and marble (Givet). The manufactures are fairly well developed ; Sedan fabrics, also blast furnaces at Givet and glass works are now in existence.

Short Account of the Operations

The Ardennes district suffered comparatively little during the war. It had to be abandoned by our troops after the defeat of Charleroi. A few stubborn fights took place here and there. Maubeuge, which was but an old fortress deprived of all modern means of defence, resisted courageously, although outnumbered by the enemy, who possessed enormous mortars. In the end the little fortress had to capitulate after several violent bombardments. General Gouraud's attack on the front of the Meuse freed a part of the Ardennes, and his troops, on their northward march along the left bank of the river, delivered heavy blows at Grand-Pré, Buzancy and Vouziers; they had reached Sedan when the armistice arrested their victorious advance.

On the right bank of the Meuse, the American army progressed jointly with our Champagne army. After having finally liberated Verdun, it captured Consenvoye, Dun-sur-Meuse and Stenay. It was about to join hands with the French army, when the Germans were obliged to ask for mercy.

In order to complete the description of this sector, we will give a general idea of the methods of the German occupation. What passed in one place was usually similar to all others, occasionally with additional cruelty when they were headed by a " junker" more tyrannical than his colleagues. When the Germans arrived in any place, the first thing they did was to occupy the Town Hall, which they converted for the Kommandantur, and posted orders to the population forbidding them to leave the town, to have lights in their houses after a certain hour (in winter 6 o'clock), and also forbidding them to leave their homes after that hour. When the soldiers were billeted, the officers and non-commissioned officers occupied all the best rooms, forcing the inhabitants to sleep on a mattress on the floor. The ordinary infantry took their quarters where they wished, pitilessly turning out old men and children. Later came the requisitions, everything

||||||||||||||||||||||||||||||||||||||||||||||||||||||||||||||||||||||||||||||||||||||||||||||||||||||||||

available being seized ; in the cellars, in the lumber-rooms and all the private houses.

Then began the painful regime of foreign occupation. Every protest made was a pretext to exact from the inhabitants high fines, sometimes amounting from 300 to 400 marks. A few girls who had gone a hundred yards or so out of a village to pluck field-flowers after the authorised hour were fined 200 marks. In order to go from one village to another it was always necessary to have a passport, and woe to the man who was met by the Germans without that precious bit of paper.

The Germans forced the inhabitants to cultivate their soil, but commandeered all the crops. Only through the American supplies, and afterwards, when that nation became a belligerent, through Spanish efforts, could the existence of these unfortunate people be secured.

The Germans continually exacted hostages, and sometimes sent them to Germany ; heavy war contributions were constantly levied on the smallest towns. In many places near the front, the men, young and old alike, sometimes young girls, were compelled to dig trenches, so that the German soldiers could shelter from the French fire. In the towns they forced the workmen to make shells which were destined to slaughter their countrymen. These poor people have suffered during the war a long and painful martyrdom. When the German authorities did consent to send back these unfortunate people to their homes, they left them with only a few rags and a little paper money, but no gold. As soon as a portion of a village had been evacuated by us, the Germans organised the pillage at their ease.

The agricultural reconstruction of all these regions will be a long process, and the Germans will never be able to pour enough gold in to repair the evil they have done. It is possible to make restitution for the material losses another man has suffered, but one cannot pay for all the physical and moral sufferings he has undergone. The time during which the inhabitants of the Ardennes were under the enemy's rule was, for them, a long series of sufferings.

War Facts

SEDAN (23,000 inhabitants) is an industrial town which has escaped disfigurement by its factories.

It was here that the first part of the 1870 war terminated (the Imperial period) by the surrender of the Chalons army and the abdication of Napoleon III. It was here the last step was taken in the world war of 1914. When, on November 11, 1918, the Armistice was signed, the American army, which had been progressing on the right bank of the Meuse, came to make its junction with the French Army, which had been progressing on the left bank of the river. Since 1871, the Germans had celebrated every year the day of Sedan (Sedantag) as a remembrance of their success of 1870. Our victory has now put an end to these manifestations.

MEZIERES.—Enclosed in a bend of the Meuse, Mézières counts but 7,000 to 8,000 inhabitants. A factory for making weighing instruments and a copper foundry are the sole activities.

CHARLEVILLE, 20,000 inhabitants is a modern town, built according to a special scheme, which by its square streets contrasts strongly with Mézières. Great industrial activity prevails here in nail works, general hardware factories, engineering work, and leather dressings. From Charleville to the frontier the Meuse is merely a broad stretch of water between two rows of factories.

It was at Charleville that the General Headquarters were established. The Kaiser first resided at the Hotel de la Gare, then, fearing our aeroplanes, he took refuge in the Villa Renaudin at Belair. In order to amuse himself, he used to cut wood in the neighbouring forest ; an incorrigible mummer, he affected, with the civilian population, as well as his officers, a sort of respectable simplicity. He seldom left Charleville, the front having no attraction for him. The Crown Prince lived with his staff at the Place Carnot. He never had an executive command, and was then leading the life of a Don Juan.

All the staff, including the Kaiser and Crown Prince trembled when our aeroplanes flew over Charleville. On April 15, 1915, our machines paid their first visit to William II and dropped five bombs near the Imperial residence. A year later a new raid of our planes found numerous victims amongst the staff.

RETHEL.—8,000 inhabitants, overlooks the Aisne. Rethel was formerly an important industrial wool centre, to-day it has but a few spinning mills, sugar factories and foundries. The church Saint-Nicolas and its entrance gate in the Renaissance style are worth seeing.

VOUZIERS.—A pretty little town of 5,000 inhabitants, built in the shape of an amphitheatre. Situated in the heart of a fertile region, Vouziers has an important agricultural market ; industry is represented only by some brickyards and sugar factories.

BUZANCY and **GRAND-PRE** offered a certain resistance when Gouraud's army was advancing in September. It was necessary to skirt these two villages, and it was only at the beginning of October that the French entered ; but these two points taken, our advance went on rapidly and our troops took in succession Rethel, Vouziers and Mézières-Charleville.

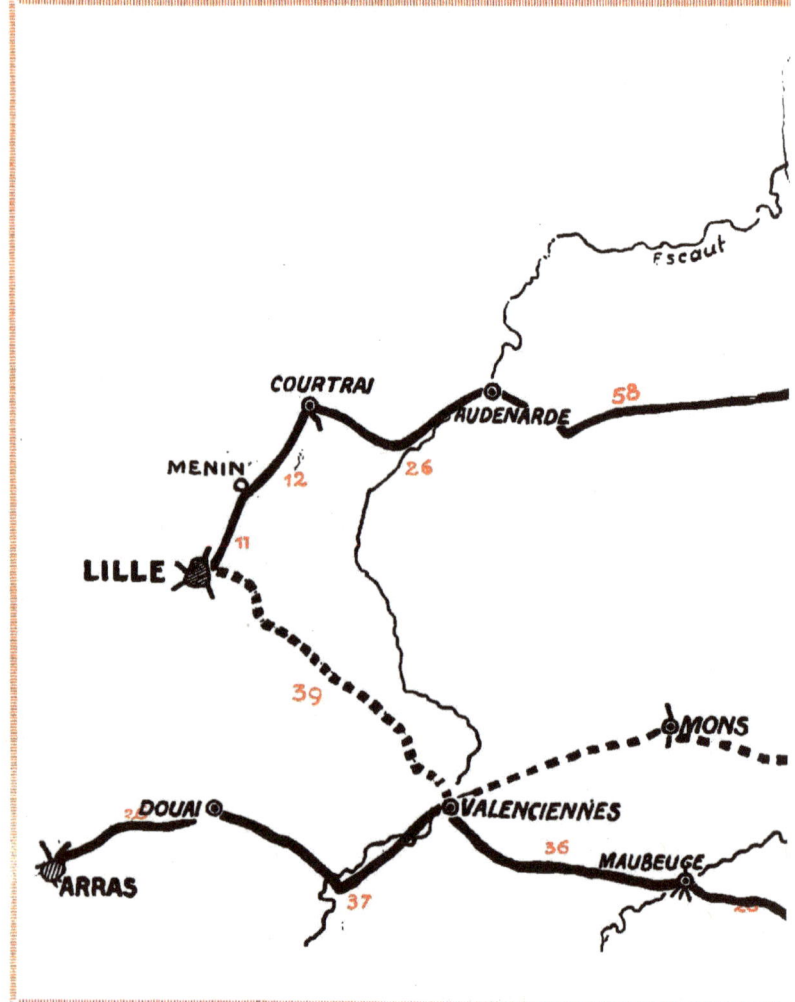

Sector 9—Belgium
Route

The tourist leaving *Lille* goes to *Courtrai*, passing *Menin*.
From Courtrai reach *Audenarde* and *Brussels*.
From Brussels visit *Malines*, and from Malines *Anvers*.
From Anvers go back to Malines through *Lierre*.

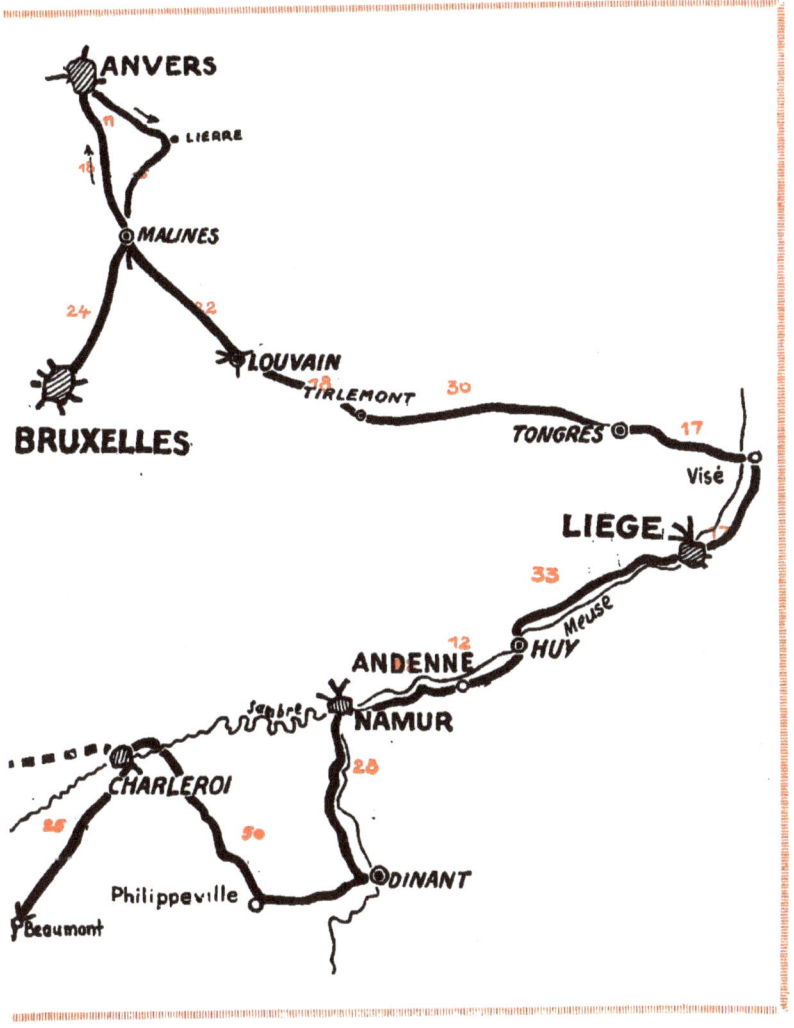

From Malines go to *Louvain*, then to *Tongres* through *Tirlemont*.

From Tongres reach the Meuse. At *Visé* go up the river to *Liège*.

After a visit to Liège, follow again the Meuse to *Dinant* through *Huy, Andenne, Namur*.

From Dinant reach *Charleroi*, through *Philippeville*.

From Charleroi reach *Valenciennes*, through *Beaumont* and *Maubeuge* or straight through *Mons*.

From Valenciennes reach Lille or *Arras* (through *Douai*).

115   II 2

HOTELS

ANTWERP

GRAND HOTEL DE LONDRES.
Avenue Keyser.

Modern comfort. First-class restaurant.

GRAND HOTEL METROPOLE.
Place Teniers.
Telegraph, Métropole.

Modern comforts.
Garage.

GRAND HOTEL TERMINUS.
In front of Central Station.
Telegraph, Anvers.   Telephone 22-36.

First-class restaurant.
Modern comfort.   Garage.

HOTEL DE LUTECE.
17 Avenue de Keyser.

Electric lighting.   Central heating.   Comfort.   Garage.

BRUSSELS

HOTEL METROPOLE.
Owners : WIELEMANS-CEUPPENS.
Boulevard Anspach.

500 rooms, with baths.
Telephone throughout.

HOTEL ASTORIA.
103 Royale.

Modern comfort.   First-class hostelry.

THE CARLTON HOTEL.
101 Avenue Louise.

First-class.   English spoken.
Modern comfort.   Garage.

GRAND HOTEL BRITANNIQUE.   Modern comfort.   Garage.
3 Place du Trône, near the Palace
and the Theatres.
Telephone, Telegraph and Post Office at the Hotel.

WILTCHER'S HOTEL.
73 Avenue Louise.
Telephone A.2600.

First-class hostelry.
150 rooms.   Modern comfort.
Family Hotel.   Garage.

HOTEL DES BOULEVARDS.
Place Charles-Rougier 2, 3, 4.
Telephone Town A-42 and A-102-24.   Province 2909.

Modern comfort.   Garage.

HOTEL DE L'ESPERANCE.
Place de la Constitution 2 to 14.
Telephone 127-91, 127-92.
Lieber's code.

Founded in 1869.
Modern comfort.
200 rooms, and apartments.
Bathrooms on all floors.

CHARLEROI

GRAND HOTEL DE L'EUROPE.
Place de la Station.
Telephone 138.

Every comfort.   Garage.

SIEBERT'S HOTEL AND RESTAURANT.
" Le Faisan Doré."
18-19 Quai de Brabant.

Modern comfort.
A.C.F.   Garage.

GRAND HOTEL.
Telephone 127 and 147.

Modern comfort.
Electricity.   Central heating.
Garage.

Sector 9—Belgium

COURTRAI

HOTEL DU NORD.
Place de la Gare.
Telephone 303.

Good kitchen.
Garage.

HOTEL ROYAL.
In front of the station.
Telephone 180.

Garage.

GHENT

HOTEL DE LA POSTA.
Place d'Armes.
Centre of town.

Every modern comfort.
100 rooms. Garage.

HOTEL GANDA.
48 Rue de Flandres.
Telephone 1050.

Comfortable rooms.
Garage 20.

HOTEL UNIVERSEL.
18 and 20 Rue de la Station.
Telephone 1.400.

English spoken. Electric
lighting. Excellent kitchen.
Garage 20.

DINANT-sur-MEUSE

HOTEL DES FAMILLES ET DE BELLEVUE.
Bellevue.
Telephone 195.

Entirely rebuilt. Modern
comfort. French, English,
German, Flemish spoken.
Cabs. Photo room.

HOTEL DE LA GARE.
Telephone 56.

Modern comfort. Garage.
Electric lighting.

LIEGE

HOTEL DE SUEDE.
Place Georges Clemenceau.
Telephone 1232.

Lift. Electricity. Central
heating. Apartments with
Bathrooms. Modern comfort.
Garage 20.

GRAND HOTEL.
Place du Maréchal Foch.
Centre of town.

All modern comforts. Lift.
Apartments with bathrooms.
Garage 50.

HOTEL DE L'EUROPE.
In front of Theatre Royal.
Here is annexed the best and most
famous restaurant of the town.

Modern comfort.
Central heating.
Garage.

HOTEL DE L'UNIVERS.
Liège-Guillemins.
Telephone 287.

Lift. 60 rooms.
Modern comfort. Bathrooms.
Garage 10.

LOUVAIN

HOTEL DE L'INDUSTRIE.
Place de la Gare.
Telephone.

Meeting-place of Motorists.
Modern comfort. Garage.
Member of T.C.B. and of the
Motor Club of Antwerp.

HOTEL MAJESTIC.
In front of the Theatre.

Comfortable rooms.
Good table. Garage.

MALINES

HOTEL DE LA COUR DE BEFFER.
22 Rue de Beffer.

First house in Malines.
Modern comfort. Garage.

MONS

GRAND HOTEL.
9 Rue de la Station.

Modern comfort.
Garage.

HOTEL DE L'ESPERANCE.
18 Rue de la Station.

Modern comfort. English
spoken. Garage.

NAMUR

HOTEL D'ARSCAMP.
Centre of town.

Modern comfort. Garage 10.
By special appointment of the
Court of Belgium and H.R.H.
Prince Napoleon.

HOTEL DE L'ANGE.

HOTEL DE FLANDRE.
In front of Station.

First-class restaurant.
Modern comfort. Garage.

Historical Account

First a Spanish possession, then an Austrian, later a French Province from 1792 to 1815, and finally tied to Holland in order to form the kingdom of the Netherlands, Belgium gained her independence in 1830. It had been declared a neutral country and it had enough courage and pride to resist Germany and to oppose itself arms in hand to the passage of the barbarous enemy. Crushed by superior numbers, it fell, and for five years lay panting under the German heel; it suffered very much, but its heroic attitude has served as an immortal memory to its King and to the Belgian nation.

Economic Account

Agriculture is not one of the important resources of Belgium, as good arable land is scarce. The country, however, is very rich in minerals, especially coal, of which 23 million tons are produced per year. Tin, lead, and iron are also found. Industry was the greatest wealth of the country, and all kinds of industry were represented, the metallurgical and mechanical industries (Charleroi, Namur, Liège), the textile industry in Flanders (laces of Louvain and Malines, cotton articles of Ghent, woollen manufactures of Antwerp, Verviers, and Liège), and several others.

Her commerce was particularly prosperous, and, owing to her geographical situation, Belgium had the largest volume of transport of all the European States. Antwerp was the great supply port for the whole of Rhenish Germany.

S. M. ALBERT　　　　　　　　　　　　**S. M. ELISABETH**

Short Account of the Operations

Belgium had been declared a neutral and independent country by the Treaty of London, 1831, and the Germans had affixed their signature to it. Their plan of campaign requiring the passage of their troops through Belgium, they sent an ultimatum to the King of Belgium requesting him to let the German troops pass through his Kingdom. King Albert, at the head of his people, was insulted at such a proposal, and swore to defend by arms the liberty and independence of Belgium. The Germans immediately entered in force ; they met at Liège an heroic resistance, which delayed their advance and allowed our troops to organise a defence more to the West. The Germans invaded almost the whole country, committing the most unheard-of crimes as a revenge for their failure before Liège. To deliver Belgium, the French General Staff attempted an offensive which, for complex reasons, failed, and eventually ended with the unfortunate retreat of Charleroi.

A visit to Belgium will be only a pilgrimage to ruins, and monuments of a sorrowful martyrdom. The Germans destroyed with a wanton violence all the masterpieces of art, heaping everywhere on the ancient Flemish soil a destruction justified only by a stupid rage to rob and kill. The Germans not only attacked objects, but they vented their rage for evil on peaceful citizens, and on women and children. Countless crimes were indulged in by the Teutonic soldiers, a fact which in itself would suffice to put Germany under the ban of the Nations. Old men and children were shot, women awfully mutilated and ill-treated. They cut the wrists of little boys, only guilty of having pointed with their fists to the murderers of their parents.

The Belgians had to suffer from the German occupation during practically the whole of the War. Against the rights of the people, they compelled the young men to make shells for the German army, and the totally unjustifiable deportations to Germany were continually multiplied. By her heroism at the beginning of the war, and by the courage with which she has borne all the rigours of the occupation, the Belgian nation has rightly deserved the admiration of the world.

War Facts

MENIN.—See Sector 10, p. 132.

BRUSSELS.—Owing to the intervention of the neutral Ambassadors and the noble behaviour of her Mayor, M. Max, this town has suffered comparatively little from the German occupation. Heavy war contributions were, however, imposed on the town, and the Mayor and several notables were deported to Germany.

It was in the neighbourhood of Brussels, on the premises of the Tir National (National Shooting Club), that Miss Cavell, the courageous English nurse, was shot for having facilitated the passage into Holland of French and Belgian soldiers concealed in the town since the German occupation. An architect, M. Bancq, who had assisted Miss Cavell in her patriotic work, was shot next morning ; he refused to be blindfolded.

MALINES.—An old Flemish town famous for her laces and old monuments, suffered very much from German barbarism. The ancient cathedral was half ruined by the shells, and numerous masterpieces of ancient art were thus destroyed. It was here that Cardinal Mercier resided, whose voice arose often above the ruins of Belgium to accuse before the whole world the savagery of the Germans.

ANTWERP was besieged at the end of August, the forts held out for a long while ; on October 7 the bombardment of the town started, and lasted until October 10, when all the forts had fallen and Antwerp had to capitulate. While the Germans entered the town with fifes and drums at the head of their troops, the unfortunate Belgians were crowded on the decks of the steamers leaving for England to escape the Prussian rule.

LOUVAIN.—The Germans, with a refinement of cruelty which can hardly be equalled, burnt the little town, and made it a sad example of the ravages of vandalism.

In the Middle Ages Louvain knew, owing to her textile industries, an era of incomparable prosperity. In 1318, Louvain had 150,000 inhabitants, the day before the war she had only 40,000. Splendid monuments had remained intact throughout the centuries, witnesses of her past grandeur ; the Town Hall, a marvel of flamboyant art, the church of Sainte-Gertrude and the Collegiate. The University contained in the Halls of Louvain a very rich library possessing a large number of precious manuscripts. All these masterpieces were burnt by order and are now only heaps of rubbish. The Germans not only destroyed the monuments but a large part of the population ; 200 civilians were shot, or perished in the fire of their houses. Thousands and thousands of poor, frightened, half-naked people left Louvain. The Germans, meanwhile, looted the private houses. In order to attempt to justify these crimes and fires, the enemy pretended that civilians had shot at their troops. In reality it was a small group of soldiers of the French rearguard, who had courageously remained in the neighbourhood of Louvain, firing at the Germans' vanguard according to military custom.

VISE.—At the head of a long list of martyred Belgian cities ; the Germans set it on fire three times and shot altogether 40 civilians.

HAECKEN.—A fierce combat took place in this town on August 12, 1914, for the control of the bridge over the Meuse. Belgian motor-cycle machine-gunners, firing at 600 yards' range, put out of action 6,000 Germans. When they did succeed in crossing the Meuse, the Belgian infantry line, previously concealed, was unmasked, and the enemy was thrown back in confusion. The German cavalry were shattered by the withering fire, the German dead covered the plain, and the standard of the Death's Head Hussars, the Crown Prince's own regiment, fell into the hands of the Belgians.

Gen. LEMAN

LIEGE.—After the Germans had accomplished their violation of Belgian neutrality they threw 120,000 men, supported by powerful heavy cannon, against the fortress of Liège. The fortress was defended by 25,000 Belgians under the command of General Léman. Their resistance was heroic ; after three days' terrible carnage, the Germans asked for a temporary cessation of hostilities to enable them to bury their dead and succour their wounded. The forts of Liège, practically razed to the ground, were forced to capitulate one after another. General Léman was the last to surrender ; bruised and blackened, he came out of a ruined redoubt, the vault of one of the casemates having eventually collapsed.

ANDENNE was burnt by the Germans on August 20, on the excuse that some of the townspeople had fired on their troops. Three hundred civilians either perished in the flames, or were shot out of hand. Von Buelow had the cynicism to publish the following proclamation afterwards : " It is with my consent that the military authorities have burnt the town of Andenne, and shot 100 citizens. I make it known to the inhabitants of Liège, in order that they may know what sort of treatment to expect at our hands."

NAMUR was defended by some elements of the French and Belgian Armies. The German bombardment destroyed the hospital, the resi-

LOUVAIN. The Town Hall

dence of the Burgomaster, the station and the prison. Two days after Namur had fallen, the Germans completely burnt the Town Hall, containing many rare collections. In the Province of Namur the enemy burnt more than 3,000 houses, and more than 1,000 people were either shot or hanged. The Germans justified these proceedings with specious arguments. The Bishop of Namur protested in these terms : " The German version of that which has passed at Namur is an odious parody of the truth. No civilian has yet been found carrying arms. The destruction by fire was not the work of an ordinary combat. They undertook the duty systematically, house by house."

DINANT.—On August 15, 1914, the Germans delivered their first attack on Dinant ; it failed, thanks to the firm resistance of the French soldiers established in the village. On the 21st the enemy returned to the attack, having received reinforcements, and, the French having evacuated the village under orders, the Germans avenged themselves for their initial check on the innocent population. They ordered all the males to collect in the square, and all the persons who had taken refuge in the environs of Liège were also gathered in or shot. They then slaughtered the assembled multitude with machine-guns. Six hundred civilians were thus massacred.

CHARLEROI has given its name to the unfortunate engagements which took place at the end of August in the Belgian Ardennes (August 22 to 24). Our troops had already taken the offensive, and, by reason of the late arrival of Headquarters orders, found themselves, in their dangerous position, inferior in numbers to the enemy ; their attack failed, and, in the face of an obstinate counter-attack, they were forced to retire. The Marne was their great opportunity to avenge this defeat.

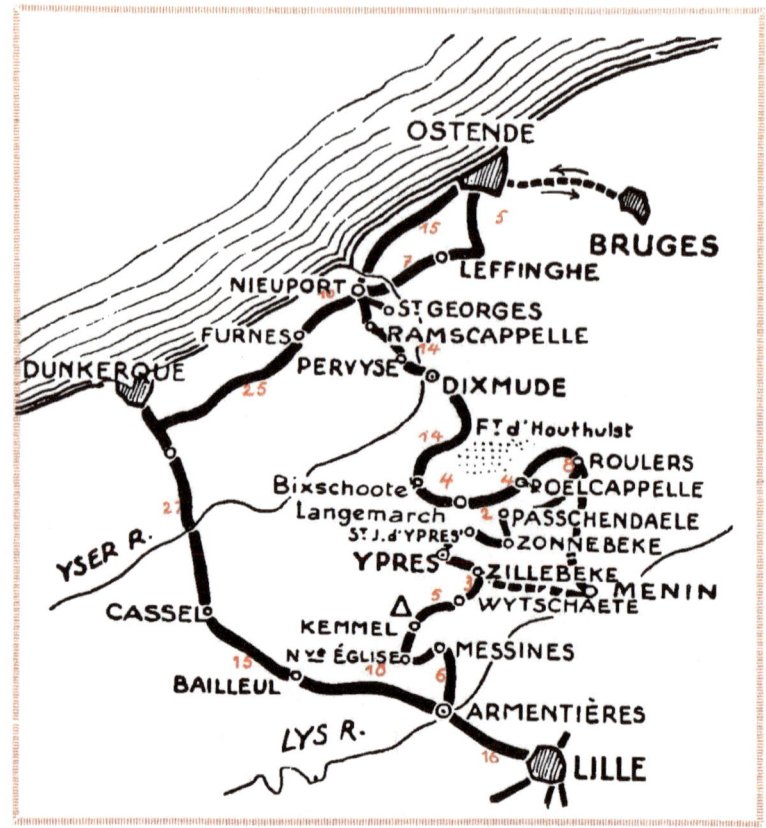

Sector 10
The Yser and Flanders Route

The tourist leaves *Lille*, and gains *Dunkirk* by way of *Armentières*, *Bailleul*, and *Cassel*. From Dunkirk follow the coast, you will see *Furnes, Nieuport,* and *Ostend.* From Ostend you may visit *Bruges*, returning to *Dixmude* and gaining Nieuport by way of *Leffinghe.*

Visit Nieuport and *Saint-Georges*, which you will find two kilomètres to the east. Then descend the Yser, taking on the way *Ramscappelle* and *Pervyse*. From Pervyse go to Dixmude. Visit Dixmude and the *Forest of Houthulst.* Return to the west and go to *Bixschoote*, and then *Roulers*, by means of *Langemarck* and *Poelcappelle*. From Roulers gain *Ypres*, passing on the way *Passchendaele, Zonnebeke* and *Saint-Jean-d'Ypres*. From Ypres the traveller should visit *Menin*. After exploring Ypres, go south by *Zillebeke* and *Wytschaete*, and so gain *Mont*

Sector 10—The Yser and Flanders Route

Kemmel. From there continue south to *Neuve-Eglise*, turn to the left and visit Messines.

From Messines return to *Lille* by way of *Armentières*.

HOTELS

BOULOGNE-SUR-MER

HOTEL DU PAVILLON IMPERIAL.
Facing the sea. Sea wall.   Every modern comfort.

HOTEL DE FOLKESTONE.   Modern comfort.
74 Quai Gambetta.   Garage.
Telephone 226.

HOTEL DE PARIS.   Modern comfort.
64 Quai Gambetta.
Telephone 0.16.

HOTEL METROPOLE AND GRILL ROOM.
27 Rue Faidherbe.
Telephone 290.

BRUGES

GRAND HOTEL.   The premier Hotel.
39 Rue St. Jacques.   Modern comfort.
Telephone 1.14 (central position).
Special motor-car meets all trains.
Garage joining Hotel (30 cars).

HOTEL DE FLANDRE.   Modern comfort.
38 Rue Nord du Sablon.   Hot water.
Recommended by Auto Clubs of   Garage.
America, France, and England.

DUNKIRK

HOTEL DES ARCADES.   All modern comforts.
Place Jean-Bart.   Motor meets all trains.
Telephone 189.   Garage.

HOTEL DU CHAPEAU ROUGE.

HOTEL DE FLANDRE AND GRAND HOTEL ANNEXE.
5 Rue St. Sebastian.   Central heating. Electric lighting. Baths. Garage.

VICTORIA HOTEL.   English spoken.
3 Quai du Risban.   Modern comfort.
Telephone 416.

LILLE

GRAND HOTEL BELLEVUE AND PALACE HOTEL.
17 Grand Place.   Modern comfort.
Motor-car and carriage service to   125 rooms. Telephone in all
the fronts, all cars fitted with   rooms. First class restaurant.
Goodrich tyres.   40 bathrooms. Garage.

HOTEL DE L'EUROPE.   Modern comfort.
30-32 Rue Basse.   Garage for 20, with repair
Telephone 801,   ditch. Court and garden.

ROYAL HOTEL.
2 Boulevard Carnot.
Telephone 29-03 ; 29-04 ; 66 inter.

Modern comfort. Garage.
American restaurant.

OSTEND
HOTEL DE LA PLAGE.
Sea-Wall.

Facing the baths. Garage.
All modern comforts.
The restaurant has a
world-wide reputation.

HOTEL SPLENDIDE.
Sea-Wall.

All modern comforts.
Sea baths. Garage.

HOTEL DE L'OCEAN.
Sea-Wall.

Modern comfort. Garage.
Open all the year round.

HOTEL KURSAAL.
Sea-Wall.
Telephone 95.

Every comfort.

ROYAL HOTEL.
Near the Breakwater.

All modern comforts. Garage.
Open all year.

HOTEL WELLINGTON.
60 Digue de Mer, at the side of the
Kursaal, facing the Baths.

Every comfort.

ROUBAIX
HOTEL CHARLES.
1 and 3 Rue de la Gare.
(The old " Hotel Moderne.")

First-class restaurant.

Historical Note

Flanders was for a long time under the domination of Spain, and
afterwards of Austria, but at the Revolution it reverted to France.
By the Treaty of 1815, however, only part remained French, the rest
was at first possessed by the Counts of Flanders, but in 1832 was
included as an integral province of Belgium.

Economic Note

The soil of Flanders is very rich ; it produces cereals, beet-root,
flax and hemp, it sustains also vast flocks and herds in its green pastures.
The industries, formerly dispersed and greatly decentralised, are now
concentrated, in a few larger towns spinning and tool-making. The
department known as the Nord, was perhaps, before the war, the
most prosperous district in all France ; abundantly provided with
navigable waterways and metalled roads ; possessing magnificent
coal mines advantageously situated close to the ports of Dunkirk
and Calais, it became an industrial region of the first order. It had
numerous spinning mills of every sort—at Lille, Roubaix, Tourcoing
and Hazebrouck—and countless engineering shops of which the most
important was " Fives-Lille " (constructing locomotives, machinery
for breweries, sugar-refineries, etc., etc.)

126

Short Account of the Operations

Ph. Sartony

Admiral RONARCH

After the Battle of the Marne was consummated by our superb victory, the Germans immediately sought to develop to the full extent the temporary advantage in the Northern Area. The French and English followed them in this celebrated "race to the sea," and eventually succeeded in so effectually stabilising their line as to render the turning movement contemplated by the enemy definitely impossible. Our front, nevertheless, was in these sectors weakly held, and in the region of the Yser the Germans instantly commenced a desperate attempt to pierce our line and gain possession of Dunkirk and Calais. From October 1914, until February 1915, the Yser sector was the scene of combats terrible in their ferocity and violence, of endurance astonishing in the awful conditions of the ground, and of a heroic bravery unsurpassed in the history of the world. Day and night the grey hordes strove ceaselessly to break down our resistance, and, in the course of the offensive, fifteen German Army Corps are computed to have been flung against the Allied lines. The Kaiser had declared that he would enter Ypres in person, and in that town would definitely proclaim the annexation of Belgium. A hitherto unexploited military weapon was then brought into use by us ; the low-lying plains of the district were converted into vast stretches of water, the dams were opened, and the Belgian people witnessed, without a murmur, the inundation of their beloved country. A severe check was thus exercised on the plans of the enemy, and many German divisions were forced to abandon the villages in which they had confidently settled down.

The spectacle of this plain, formerly so fertile, prosperous, and picturesque, now an immense and practically uninterrupted waste of waters, is appalling. The hideous, noxious mud of the swamps, rises continuously ; it invades the trenches, it submerges them, very often both armies are compelled to abandon their front lines, it is all-pervading. Rain falls ceaselessly, and these awful weather conditions, coupled with the intense cold and bad accommodation, invariably result in fever, frost-bite, and a consequently high death-rate. It was said that at this time men came to disregard the shells, and think only of their dug-outs.

The sacrifice performed had, however, its expected results. The fronts became stable, the enemy's attack failed, and this small district, the only remaining part of Belgium, rested permanently in Allied hands.

On July 31, 1917, the English troops took the offensive and cleared Ypres of the enemy, in spite of numerous counter-attacks which lasted for a whole fortnight. The British Army also retook, on September 20 and 26, Inverness Wood and Zonnebeke ; in six days they captured over 9,000 prisoners. In October the advance was arrested before the Forest of Houthulst and the hills East of Passchendaele ; nevertheless, in four months the English and French had taken more than 30,000 prisoners, and the German High Command had thrown in 600,000 soldiers to fill the breach.

On April 9, 1918, intoxicated by their success in the South, the Germans launched a formidable offensive on both sides of the Lys river.

They succeeded in approaching Ypres, but could not progress rapidly enough to have any hope of taking it. The German line then formed a salient, with the apex projecting between Ypres and Givenchy up to the western outskirts of Bailleul and Merville. This salient was reduced by the Allied armies in their attack of September 5, 1918. Ypres was finally relieved of all danger, and the English, French, and American forces advanced side by side to the onslaught. From September 27 to October 4 we penetrated to a depth of nine miles on a 25-mile front ; 10,500 prisoners and 350 guns fell into our hands.

War Facts

LILLE.—Lille was before the War a prosperous city of 23,000 inhabitants. Her economic wealth consisted mainly of the textile and engineering industries ; she possessed a famous university, and divers technical colleges. Immediately after the Revolution Lille sustained a terrible siege during the year 1792, and the Convention announced that Lille " had justly merited the admiration and gratitude of her country." She deserved no less praise during the late War for the magnificent spirit she displayed during the German occupation.

For various reasons the High Command judged it advisable to evacuate Lille after the Battle of Charleroi. During October 2 and 3, 1914, the Germans occupied the city, and the means they employed seem so extraordinary as to be worthy of description. On October 2 the population observed a closed motor car enter the Market Place of the town, from whence descended a German officer and four soldiers. They went first to the Town Hall and there proclaimed the town invested. Under menace of their revolvers the Mayor was forced to deliver a large sum of money as a " War Contribution." For two days they terrorised the town, collecting arms and posting proclamations.

Our troops then reoccupied Lille, but their strength was small, and on October 12 and 13 the enemy advanced to the assault. The French force only possessed two field guns ; but by dint of constantly changing their position and transporting them from one bastion to another, they managed to give the Germans an illusory idea of their resources. A French aeroplane on the 13th dropped messages on the market-place announcing the welcome news of approaching reinforcements. These reinforcements, however, did not arrive, and on the 14th the Germans penetrated into the town. They signalised their success by completely destroying by fire four of the principal quarters of the town. Bombs were also thrown into the cellars in which the terrified inhabitants had taken refuge. Of the brave military defenders, some were killed, some were taken prisoners, and others, but a few, lived on in the town disguised as civilians. A certain master-builder named Jacquet, by heroic efforts succeeded in passing two or three hundred of these men into Holland, from whence they rejoined the French Army ; he was eventually denounced as a traitor and shot.

During their occupation, the Germans committed thousands of exactions. They first extorted large sums from the population as " War Contribution," payable only in gold. They requisitioned, with no warning or compensation, provisions of all sorts ; their ruthless methods even extended as far as commandeering the hospital mattresses as well as those of private dwelling houses. But the most terrible of all their crimes was the melancholy deportation order of April 16, 1916. At three o'clock in the morning machine-guns were established in all the principal streets ; they set fire to the Town Hall, and, while it was burning, soldiers entered all the houses, and selected a certain number of women and girls for deportation. The trembling and panic-stricken victims were then assembled, forming a party of some 7,000 or 8,000, and, surrounded by a detachment of troops, were marched away to exile. When they were not engaged in repairing trenches, many of them suffered horrible degradations and hundreds disappeared. After four years' martyrdom Lille was at last delivered by the English on October 17, 1918.

DUNKIRK.—This town, before the war, was one of our most flourishing ports, and a rapid development was proceeding in its trade, which could not, perhaps, have been approached in all France.

Following the German offensive, having as one of its main objectives the capture of this town, the port was subjected to a long and indiscriminate bombardment by air, sea and land. The maritime commerce of the port was necessarily somewhat interrupted, but it still served as a useful base for torpedo-boat flotillas and submarine chasers.

The guns which bombarded Dunkirk had a range of 24 miles ; they fired a shell of 381 mm. in diameter, weighing 2,072 lbs.

OSTEND.—Formerly a fashionable watering-place, this town served for some time as the German U-boat Base. On April 23, 1918, the English executed a naval raid of splendid daring against this den of pirates. The obsolete cruiser " Vindictive " was specially fitted out for this operation. A similar attempt was made previously at Zeebrugge, and gained a marvellous success. An old submarine charged with explosive rammed the Mole and was blown up, partly cutting the Mole in two ; two vessels were sunk in the channel and obstructed the passage, and innumerable deeds of heroism were performed during the desperate combats which took place. The raid did not succeed so well at Ostend, a light wind dispersing the smoke screen designed to cover the movements of the attacking squadron, and the operation was temporarily suspended. It was once more undertaken on the night of May 9 and 10. The "Vindictive" succeeded in entering the channel, and after a frightful battle with the shore artillery, during which a large part of her complement were killed, was effectively sunk in the main passage, and the desired object attained.

BRUGES.—Bruges is an old Flemish town of 55,000 inhabitants well known for its ancient monuments ; it is the birthplace of the celebrated painter Van Eyck, a certain number of whose masterpieces still remain in the town.

Some beautiful lace is woven in the old city, which is distinguished for its calm and placid air of gentle melancholy.

NIEUPORT.—This town sustained its first bombardment on October 17, 1914, and, a large number of the population still wishing to remain in spite of the imminent danger of a German occupation, they were evacuated by force. A battle took place around this town, lasting for a long while, and in which an English squadron of cavalry gave valuable assistance to our Army. An English naval officer solicited the favour of being allowed to defend Nieuport with his company of machine-guns. This was granted, and he established himself in an advantageous position before the town. After a stubborn fight, the town was taken and he and his men killed, but he had achieved his purpose ; twenty-four hours had elapsed since the commencement of the combat and the delay was sufficient.

DIXMUDE.—The village was defended by the Marines of Admiral Ronarc'h, composed mainly of Bretons, inured to suffering, who fought like lions, and only succumbed to pressure of superior numbers. On October 24, 1914, the enemy bombarded Dixmude with incendiary shells, and a great part of the village was still burning when the battle took place.

THE YSER RIVER AND CANAL.—Around this little river many bloody fights took place, in which our men, surrounded by mud, and drenched with rain, resisted valiantly, often one against ten. On November 11, 1914, a German colonel advanced to the attack of the bridge of Dry Crachten, on the Yser Canal, holding in front of his regiment some captured Zouaves ; the French charged with the defence of the west bank dared not fire, until an old Zouave cried to them from the enemy's ranks : "Fire ! my lads, fire !" They let loose a volley then, and laid dead on the ground the noble prisoners and the first lines of the enemy.

LA MAISON DU PASSEUR.—"In front of Poescle, and midway between Dixmude and Ypres, we succeeded at last in conquering a

130

ferryman's house, which had been violently disputed for at least a month ; and the enemy had without success attempted to deprive us of our capture by heavy artillery bombardment."

It was thus that an official communiqué related the capture of the Maison du Passeur. In official language it could not do justice to all the carnage and horror which had taken place. Our soldiers attacked in mud up to the waist. The Germans defended the little house with an unprecedented tenacity. Finally our troops carried it by assault ; la Maison du Passeur, taken and retaken dozens of times, rested definitely in our hands—it was no more than a mass of bricks and cinders.

Ph. Antony

YPRES. The Hall

HOUTHULST FOREST.--This was the culminating point of the progress of the Anglo-French offensive on November 1917. The troops of General Anthoine fought valiantly, but all their efforts failed to dislodge the enemy, who, aided by the broken nature of the terrain, opposed an obstinate resistance.

POELCAPPELLE AND PASSCHENDAELE. — These two villages, which we had captured in 1917, had to be abandoned during the German offensive of 1918, the British General Staff fearing that the Ypres salient would otherwise be encircled. The enemy, emboldened by this bloodless victory, had strong hopes of effecting the capture of

Ypres, and instantly threw 120,000 men to the attack in this sector, but all to no purpose.

YPRES.—In the middle ages this ancient town had a magnificent military reputation, and in 1914 there yet existed several splendid monuments of its former grandeur ; in particular, the Cloth Hall, which is considered a masterpiece of its kind, the Cathedral and the Town Hall. For month after month the Germans cast division on division into the field of carnage in a vain effort to gain the town. They even pretended to disregard the destruction their bombardment wrought among its magnificent examples of ancient architecture. One of their Generals attempted to justify their action. " Of what importance are these ancient edifices," he wrote, " in comparison with the urgent need of victory for our arms ? " An officer of German artillery boasted of having fired over sixty shots at the belfry of the Cathedral. Thanks to the bravery of our soldiers, Ypres itself never fell into the power of the Germans ; and during the whole war it remained the capital of ruined Belgium.

MENIN.—This town was captured for our arms in the Anglo-Belgian attack of September 27–28, 1918. The Houthulst Forest had been cleared in two days. The Belgians were in the environs of Roulers ; the English, with whom were incorporated several American divisions, had menaced Menin for some days, when finally it fell to their assault.

MONT KEMMEL.—Mont Kemmel is a small hill 500 feet high, but it dominates the whole of the Flanders plain, and constitutes in itself an excellent observation post. Its possession was sharply disputed in the course of every offensive, both German and Allied.

Mont Kemmel was for the first time taken by the Germans in their offensive of April 1918, against Armentières and Hazebrouck. To attempt the capture of the chain of hills which extends to the west of Mont Kemmel 100,000 Germans advanced to the attack. After practically surrounding Kemmel, they succeeded in encircling a French regiment, which, after fighting heroically was compelled to surrender. The resistance being thus weakened, Kemmel was abandoned, though not without stubborn contests. On August 31, 1918, however, a strong English patrol once more regained possession. They methodically progressed in short rushes, first an advance on the right, then on the left; and the enemy, threatened by a flanking movement, eventually abandoned the combat. Many American divisions, by their superb élan, contributed in no small degree to the success of the manœuvre.

MESSINES.—This town was first taken by the English on June 7 and 8, 1917, after a tremendous artillery preparation. The hill on which Messines lies had been previously organised by the enemy for defence ; it was covered with defensive posts armoured in bullet-proof concrete, in addition to the usual trench-lines, redoubts, and machine-gun posts ; underground dug-outs also abounded. To overthrow this seemingly invulnerable position, the English accomplished the enormous task of tunnelling directly under the crest of the hill 19 galleries for mines. The artillery preparation lasted seven entire days; and at seven o'clock on the morning of the attack the 19 mines were simultaneously exploded, killing and maiming great numbers of the enemy. The infantry then advanced to the assault, preceded and covered by low-flying aeroplanes which constantly machine-gunned the few remaining defenders of the trench line. In one rush the crest was taken, on June 8 progress was made as far as the Commines Canal, and all counter-attacks beaten off. Seven thousand prisoners, 47 guns, and 60 trench mortars were taken.

Messines was recaptured by the Germans in their offensive of April 9, 1918; and finally delivered by General Plumer, operating in concert with the Belgian Army, which was, at this crowning phase of its glorious career, commanded by King Albert in person.

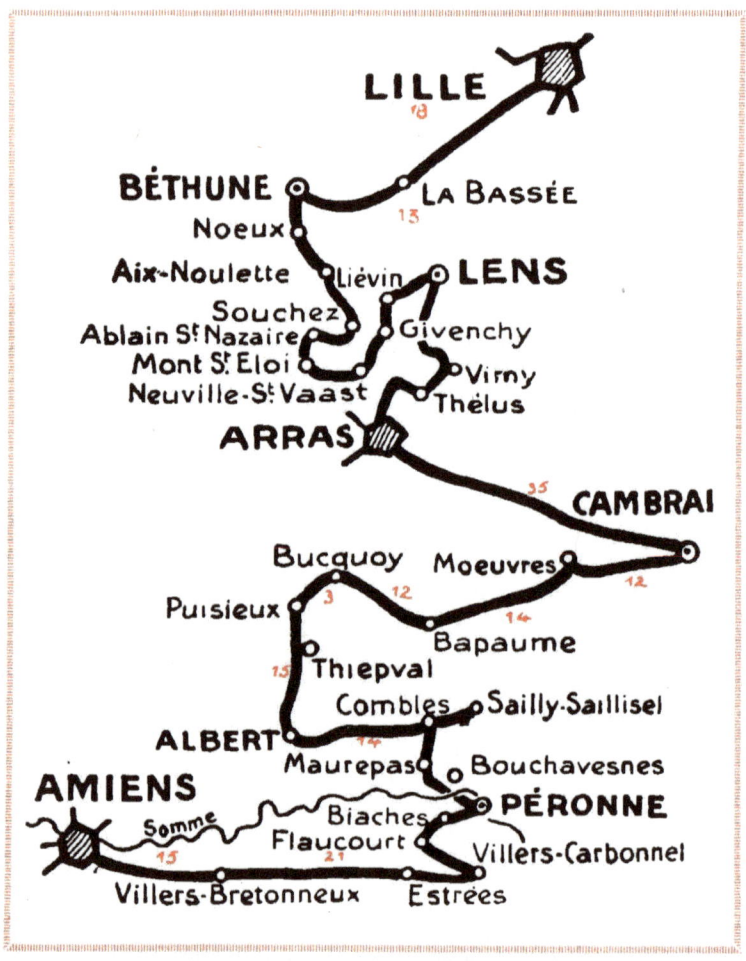

Sector 11—Artois

Route

The tourist departs from *Lille* and takes the direction of *Béthune* by way of *La Bassée.*

From Béthune he takes the Arras road, visits *Nœux-les-Mines*, *Aix Noulette*, until he comes to *Souchez*, here he turns to the right to see *Ablain-Saint-Nazaire*; at Ablain he turns to the left and descends on *Mont-Saint-Eloi*, by *Carency*; at Mont-Saint-Eloi he again turns to the left, crosses the main road at *La Targette*, visits *Neuville-Saint-Vaast* and *Givenchy*, then gains *Lens* by way of *Angres* and *Liérin*.

Visit Lens. Then take the road Lens-Arras. Make a slight détour to the left to visit *Vimy* and *Thélus*, then go to Arras. After visiting Arras, drive to *Cambrai* by the main road. Having seen Cambrai, gain *Bapaume*, making a slight circuit so as to see *Mœuvres*.

From Bapaume go to *Bucquoy*, then descend to *Albert*, making on the way, at *Hamel*, another détour on the left to see *Thiepval*.

After visiting Albert, continue to *Combles*; at two and a half miles from Combles have a glance round *Sailly-Saillisel*, an interesting spot.

From Sailly-Saillisel resume the Combles road, go down to *Maurepas* and *Cléry*, then gain *Boucharesnes* and from thence *Péronne*. After a visit to Péronne, turn to the right at the Paris gate and see *Biaches*, then by way of *Flaucourt* and *Barleux* gain the main road to *Villers-Carbonnel*, and so onwards to *Amiens* by *Villers-Bretonneux*.

HOTELS

ABBEVILLE

BULL'S HEAD HOTEL.
44 Rue St. Gilles.

First-class restaurant.
Garage.

AMIENS

RHINE HOTEL.
4 Rue du Noyon.

Every comfort.
Garage with ditch.
American bar.   Garden.

UNIVERSAL HOTEL.
2 Rue du Noyon.

Modern comfort.   Garage.

HOTEL DE LA PAIX.
15 Rue Dumeril.

Every comfort.   Garage.

COMMERCIAL HOTEL.
32 Rue des Jacobins.

Every comfort.   Garage.

ARRAS

· COMMERCIAL HOTEL.
Rue Gambetta.

Every comfort.   Garage.

CALAIS

HOTEL DU SAUVAGE.
39 Rue Royale, 41.
Telephone 1.11.

Modern comfort.

METROPOLE HOTEL.
Place de la Gare.
Telephone 4.95.

Modern comfort.   Garage.

TERMINUS HOTEL.
Near the landing-stage.

Sea view.   Landing stage.
Calais-Dover Terminus.

HOTEL MEURICE.
7 and 9 Rue de Guise.
Telephone 1.30.

Modern comfort.
Skating rink.

CENTRAL HOTEL.
(Station Buffet, Calais Town.)

Modern comfort.

CAMBRAI

HOTEL DU MOUTON BLANC, ET HOTEL MODERNE
RENUIS.   First-class restaurant.
5 Rue d'Alsace-Lorraine.   Garage.
Telephone.

DOUAI

HOTEL DU GRAND CERF.   Modern fittings and comfort.
20 Rue St. Jacques.   Garage.
Telephone 41.

VALENCIENNES

FLANDERS HOTEL.   First-class restaurant.
2 Rue de la Halle.   Plain cooking.
    Motor garage.
    Modern comfort.

SAINT OMER

GRAND COMMERCIAL HOTEL.   Modern comfort.
Telephone 13.   Bath-rooms.
    Central heating.
    Garage with ditch.

GRAND HOTEL.   Modern comfort.   Garage.
60 Rue de Dunkerque.
Telephone.
GRAND HOTEL DE FRANCE.   Up-to-date installation.
Grande-Place.   Central heating.
Telephone 62.   Electric lighting.
    Garage.

Historical Account

Artois was declared a French province in the fifteenth century, but was several times reconquered by the Dutch and Spanish. It was not until the eighteenth century that this district became definitely French. We find in the old towns of Artois many curious remains of the Spanish occupation.

Economic Account

Artois is rather more an industrial and mining region than an agricultural one. Nevertheless, agriculture has attained some degree of prosperity. Besides growing cereals and beetroot, they breed horses on a large scale. It is from the Artois soil that the largest quantity of coal in France is extracted (mining centres of Courrières, Nœux, Marles, Liévin). Unfortunately, the war has ruined this once prosperous region, and the mines especially will need some years of painstaking work in order to reproduce the pre-war output. Industry is represented by numerous foundries and forges. Sugar-mills for the treatment of beet-root are everywhere established throughout the country. There are also a few paper mills and leather factories.

Short Account of the Operations

Marshal DOUGLAS HAIG

Gen. BYNG

The famous points of this region are chiefly the villages and ridges obstinately contested during our two offensives of 1915 on May 9 and September 25.

On May 9 our infantrymen, after a long artillery preparation, stormed the enemy's positions in the region of Ablain-Saint-Nazaire. The first days of the attack gave splendid results, but on the third our first shock was exhausted before Neuville-Saint-Vaast and Souchez. 10,000 prisoners, however, remained in our hands, and seven villages were redeemed from the enemy.

Four months later, another offensive was launched, on September 25, in co-operation with that in Champagne. After a few successes, our troops stopped, this attack having been only a diversion to the real one in Champagne.

In 1917, the British took Vimy and Liévin and approached very near to Lens.

The ground so hardly won by the French and British armies had to be abandoned at the time of the German offensive at the end of March 1918. It was retaken by the British division of General Byng in September and October 1918. Lens, which up to that time had resisted all attacks, was taken without fighting. Douai and Cambrai fell shortly afterwards.

The struggles in this sector always had an extremely violent character; the British, and particularly the Canadians, gained in these " death corners " numberless titles of glory.

The battle of which we shall now speak took place in 1916, and is called " The Battle of the Somme." It would have been difficult to have included the theatre of this battle in Sector 12.

On July 3, 1916, in order to reply to the German attack on Verdun, and show the enemy that Verdun was not, as he had declared, " the tomb of the French army," our troops went " over the top " and our attacks starting from Albert brought us in the end to the outskirts of Combles and Péronne.

137

Sector 11—Artois

|||||||||||||||||||||||||||||||||||||||||||||||||||||||||||||||||||||||||||||||||||||||||||||||||||||||||||||||||||||||||||||||||||||||||||||||
From July 1 to 20 the Allies advanced ten kilomètres on a front of forty kilomètres, making 20,000 prisoners and seizing 140 guns. The struggle was protracted until January 1917, and heavy fighting was experienced on ground so muddy that our soldiers often could not dig any trenches. At the end of March 1917, the Germans, retreating on the Oise, abandoned the southern part of the battlefields as well as Péronne.

It was during the battle of the Somme that the British the first time employed a new weapon whose general adoption later gave marvellous results—the tank. The first of its kind was the famous "Crème de Menthe." It engendered a panic in the German lines before Flers.

War Facts

LA BASSEE was famous for the bloody attacks and counter-attacks of 1915. The town was taken and retaken several times. At the time of their March 1918 offensive, the Germans once more got hold of it, and it was ultimately reconquered by an American division at the end of September.

The region of **NŒUX - LES - MINES, AIX - NOULETTE - SOUCHEZ, NEUVILLE-SAINT-VAAST** was the scene of our offensive of May 9, 1915. Our attack, executed after an artillery preparation of three days, progressed rapidly in the beginning, but was arrested before the defences of Neuville-Saint-Vaast and Souchez. The first of these villages was taken by desperate fighting, house to house, cellar after cellar; there was terrible hand-to-hand fighting with grenades. We were at that time making use of bottles filled with melinite and fitted with a detonator. Our troops could not carry Souchez in spite of magnificent efforts ; they succeeded in taking the sugar-mills, but the village itself remained in the hands of the Germans. Near Notre-Dame-de-Lorette there was a famous factory "The White Way." Our Colonials succeeded in getting hold of it, despite an obstinate defence. At the outskirts of Notre-Dame-de-Lorette, on May 9, we made 1,000 prisoners and the Germans lost 3,000 men.

LENS was the object of several offensives. The capture of Lens was one of the immediate aims of our offensive of 1915. On August 15, 1917, Lens was encircled by the Canadian troops, who secured a certain number of the workmen's quarters in the neighbourhood of the town. The two roads, that of Lille and that of Douai, though continually shelled by the artillery, remained in the hands of the Germans. The possession of Lens was, nevertheless, of no strategic utility to them. The town was taken by us only at the end of September 1918. Lens was formerly the centre of an important mining industry ; the pits have particularly suffered from artillery fire and the systematic destruction of the Germans.

Sector 11—Artois

VIMY.—The Vimy Ridge was taken by the British on April 9 and 10, 1917. It had already resisted four French attacks. The enemy had organised in its development all the art of military defence; the British, in order to get hold of Vimy Ridge, had brought into action 4,000 guns for seven days, firing about ten millions of shells. It rained all the time of the preparation. The attack started from the line of Angres, La Folie Farm, east of Neuville-Saint-Vaast. La Folie Farm, Thélus, Givenchy-en-Gogelle, were taken in one rush. On the 10th Vimy was taken. In two days the British captured 11,000 prisoners and 100 guns.

ARRAS was not occupied by the Germans in 1914. In spite of their determination, they could never get hold of the old Artois capital. They sought to take revenge for their failure by systematically destroying the town. The finest monuments, the Town Hall and its belfry, the Cathedral, the picturesque Esplanade, are all in ruins. The battle lines passed through the town suburbs, and there were frequently violent struggles. The British, in March and April 1917, succeeded in entering Arras, and pursuing the enemy about 6 miles as far as Arleux, and Monchy-le-Preux. The splendid victory of Vimy released the North of Arras.

Ph. Léen

ARRAS
La Chapelle des Ursulines

CAMBRAI was delivered from German domination on October 10, 1918. A fine effort for her redemption had been attempted at the end of November 1917, by the British General Byng. For the first time a method of attack was employed which in 1918 brought us such fine victories.

The south-west sector of Cambrai was occupied only by troops tired and relatively weak in fighting strength. A British attack was prepared in great secrecy, and on November 20, in the morning, covered by a moving barrage, a squadron of 150 to 200 tanks pushed forward, followed by the infantry.

The British reached Fontaine-Notre-Dame, 4 miles from Cambrai, Noyelle, Marcoing, and Crève Cœur. They took 11,500 prisoners and 136 guns. Unfortunately, their reserve troops were not sufficiently strong to break up two formidable German counter-attacks on November 30, the one to the north and the other to the south of the Cambrai salient. The British could not hold their ground, and brought in a French army corps. A large part of the ground conquered previously by General Byng was thus lost.

BAPAUME, taken by the Germans at the time of our retreat in August 1914, was evacuated in March 1917, during their strategic retreat. The Town Hall, under which they had placed a delay mine, was blown up ten days later, swallowing in the explosion two French deputies. Bapaume was taken from us once more at the time of the German offensive of March 21, 1918, but on August 29, having outflanked the town, the Allies got hold of it in a few hours.

SAILLY-SAILLISEL was taken on October 15 and 18, 1916. The village was attacked from three sides at the same time. This position was extremely important for the Germans, therefore they attempted numerous counter-attacks in order to capture it, but without success.

The fighting was prolonged and bitter in this murderous corner, and at the end of December struggles in the mud and under fearful weather conditions were still in progress.

BOUCHAVESNES was taken practically in one bound. The reserve troops on September 12, 1917, at 17.30 p.m., got the order to attack; at 17.45 they were marching to the front line; at 18.30 they attacked : " Order of attacking, a thunder-clap," writes an officer. The success was no less rapid. The three objects were taken without stopping. A battalion commanding officer sent this remarkable bulletin : " I am occupying the village; first objective taken splendidly, second also, the third will be in our hands within four minutes ; extend the range."

The Germans reacted, but their counter-attacks were broken by our infantry fire.

PERONNE suffered excessively through the war. Uncovered by the Germans' retreat of March 1917, she once more experienced invasion a year later, at the time of the big German offensive against General Gough's troops. When our soldiers entered in 1917, the town was thoroughly looted, and almost all the inhabitants had been deported. Some delay action mines left by the Germans exploded and caused many deaths.

BIACHES was taken by our infantry on July 9, 1916 ; a little fort, organised in the town itself, of which but a heap of formless rubbish was left, was taken by one bound. Nine French soldiers took prisoner 113 Bavarians concealed at the bottom of a trench.

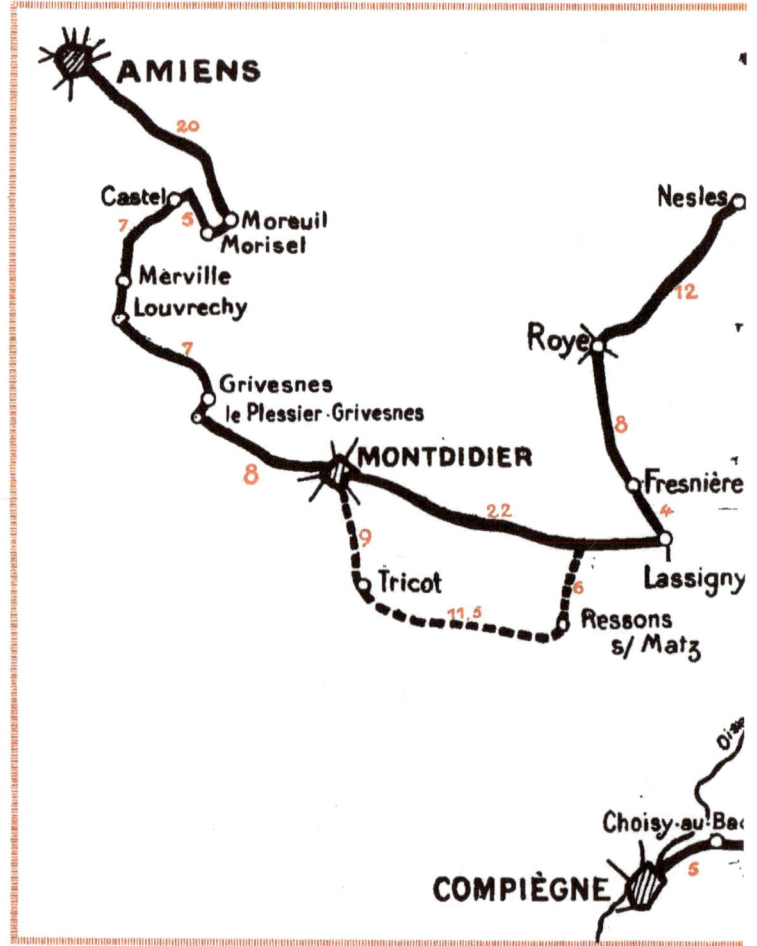

Sector 12—Picardy
Route

The tourist will leave *Amiens* and follow the road Amiens-Mont-didier till *Moreuil*. Visit Moreuil, then pass to *Morisel*, there turn to the right, take first parallel road and go to *Castel*. From Castel go to *Merville, Louvrechy*, then on the Montdidier road to *Grivesnes*. A small detour in order to see *le Plessier-Grivesnes*, and from there reach *Montdidier*. Visit Montdidier. From Montdidier reach *Lassigny*.

The tourist will, from Montdidier, drive to *Tricot*, and there, turning to the left, reach *Ressons-sur-Matz* and Lassigny; he will be able to see

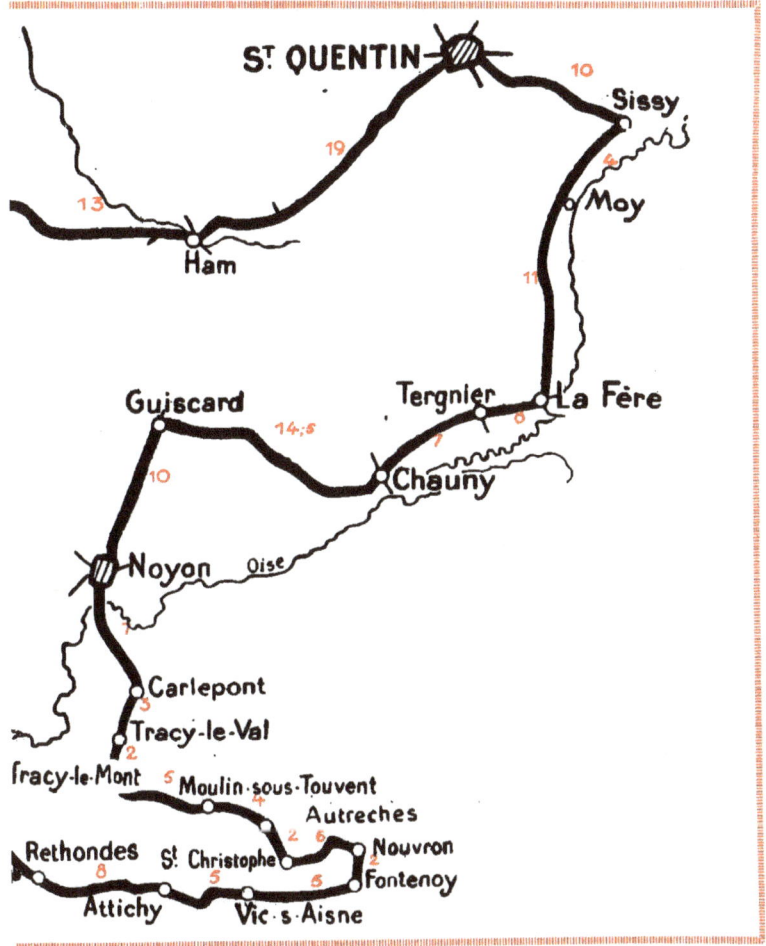

the spots where the German attack on June 9, 1918, was broken and from whence our courageous counter-attacks started on the 12th. From Lassigny turn to the north, reach *Roye* ; there turn to the right, and through *Nesles* and *Ham* go to *Saint-Quentin*.

From Saint-Quentin, reach the Oise at *Sissy*, and turning to the right, go to *Moy* and *La Fère*. From La Fère, coming back to the west, pass to *Tergnier* and *Chauny* ; there turn to the north in order to see *Guiscard* and from there reach *Noyon*.

After visiting Noyon descend, following approximately the old front line, *Carlepont*, *Tracy-le-Val*, *Tracy-le-Mont*, *Moulin-sous-Touvent*,

Autrèches, Saint-Christophe, and *Nouvron.* At the latter, turn to the right. At *Fontenoy* take the route of Soissons-Compiègne to the north of the Aisne and reach *Compiègne* through *Vic-sur-Aisne, Attichy, Rethondes, Choisy-au-Bac* and Compiègne.

Hotels

BEAUVAIS

GRAND HOTEL DE FRANCE ET D'ANGLETERRE.
Telephone 1.07.   Modern comfort.
                                          Auto-garage in the Hotel.
                                          Mechanician attached to the
                                            house.
                                          A.A., A.C.F., T.C.F.
                                          English spoken.
HOTEL DE L'ECU.   Comfort. Garage.
Telephone 1.88.

COMPIEGNE

HOTEL DU ROND-ROYAL.   Latest comfort. Garage.
At the entrance of the wood.   Splendid view.
PALACE HOTEL.   Modern comfort.
Place du Palais.   Large garden.
Telephone 115.   American bar. Garage.
HOTEL DE LA CLOCHE.   Garage. A.C.F.
Place de l'Hôtel de Ville.
Telephone 85.

SAINT-QUENTIN

HOTEL MODERNE ET DU COMMERCE.
27 Rue du Palais de Justice.   Garage.
HOTEL DE FRANCE ET D'ANGLETERRE.
28 Rue Emile-Zola.   Garage.

Historical Account

Picardy, one of the earliest French provinces, whose fidelity had been praised as far back as the fourteenth century. The inhabitants of Picardy then spoke a special dialect, of which several words have remained in the present language of the peasants of this region. In the seventeenth century Picardy was the theatre of violent struggles; in 1870, during the German invasion, a heavy battle was engaged in by our northern army at Bapaume.

Economic Account

Picardy is a fertile region where corn, beetroot, and potatoes are grown under the most modern conditions. Industry is in course of development, particularly the textile industry. The most important manufactures are flax, hemp and cotton, carpets and hosiery. There are also a few foundries and engineering shops.

Ph. Sartony
Gen. DEBENEY

Ph. Sartony
Gen. MAISTRE

Ph. Meley
Gen. PELLE

Short Account of the Operations

From the end of the Marne battle till spring 1917, the battle line passed approximately through Péronne, Chaulnes, Roy, Lassigny, Ribecourt, Nouvron, Soissons. On March 17, 1917, while a Franco-British offensive was being actively prepared on this front, the Germans accomplished a strategic retreat and withdrew to a line passing west of Saint-Quentin, Roye, La Fère, and the forest of Saint-Gobain. During this retreat the Germans devastated the regions they were abandoning. A Berlin paper writes : " The abandoned ground forms an actual desert which one could name the kingdom of death." The fruit-trees were sawn down, the Germans blew up the houses with dynamite, villages and towns were burnt down, and altogether 214 villages, 225 churches, and 37,000 houses were reduced to ruins. And this region had not finished with the Germans yet.

On March 21, 1918, the German army, reinforced by more than a million men from the Russian front, attacked on a line of 50 miles, from Arras to the forest of Saint-Gobain. The shock-troops, 900,000 men in all, had been transferred, in the greatest secrecy, from the Ardennes, to the sector of attack. At 2 o'clock in the morning, the Germans started a fearful bombardment, followed by gas clouds. A thick fog assisted their plans. General Gough's troops fought one against three, and inflicted heavy losses upon the enemy, but they were not able to hold out before such masses, so they gave way ; many of them were made prisoners, and a great number retired. In a few days the Germans had recaptured all the ground abandoned at the end of March 1917. They even passed the old line, got hold of Montdidier, and were preparing to take Amiens, when the arrival of reinforcements relieved the situation and arrested the enemy on the ridges overlooking the Avre. Ludendorff had sacrificed, from March 21 to April 4, in order to get this appreciable but not decisive result, 250,000 men ; from March 21 to 31 he had thrown into the battle 1,200,000 soldiers.

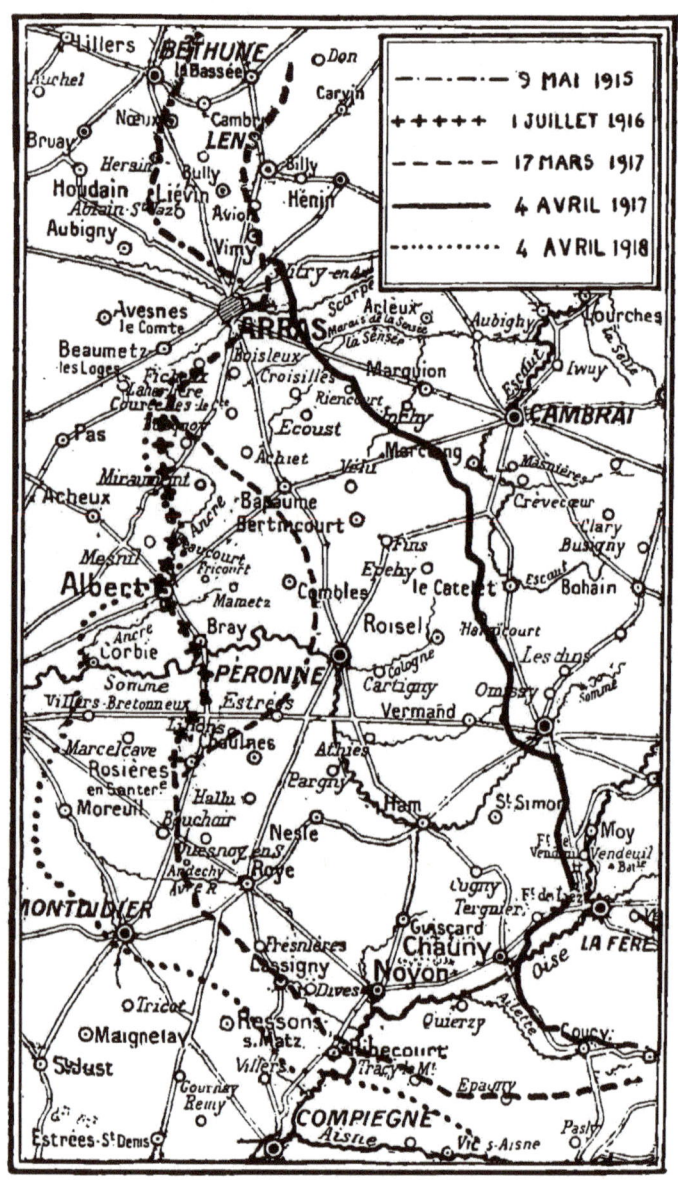

BATTLES OF THE SOMME AND PICARDY

Up to May 1, the Germans had seized from the Allies 127,000 prisoners and 1,600 guns. We had to suffer still another heavy defeat at the Chemin-des-Dames, and the enemy could now believe himself near to success, but he did not count on the heroism of the French troops and the gallantry of the American reinforcements now disembarking daily.

On June 9, 1918, in the region of Matz, the enemy attempted an advance on Compiègne. He succeeded in progressing from 5 to 7 miles, but was arrested not far from Compiègne by a flank counter-attack of Mangin's army.

The British and French took a splendid revenge on August 6, 1918. The British army, under Rawlinson, attacked after an hour of violent shelling, the infantry progressing behind a terrible rolling barrage fire. It was a surprise for the enemy, the tanks got in the rear of the infantry, destroying the machine-guns, dug-outs, and throwing panic in the German lines.

Debeney's French army was advancing in similar conditions, preceded by Renault's tanks. They took by surprise some Germans in the very act of harvesting, and the artillery men were made prisoners before they could reach their guns. Armoured cars caused great confusion amongst the German staffs. On August 10 Montdidier was taken; General Humbert in his turn attacked in the region of the Matz, and progressed rapidly. On the 13th, the Germans had lost in this region 32,000 prisoners (amongst whom were 8 colonels), 650 guns, thousands of machine-guns, three complete trains, and we reconquered Bapaume, Péronne, Chaulnes, Foye, Noyon. The advance then became slower, but on October 6 we were on the line of Saint-Quentin and soon we passed the Oise. Saint-Quentin was taken, and on November 11 the enemy was almost at the frontier.

War Facts

AMIENS was only held by the Germans at the beginning of the war for a few days, and, in spite of his efforts, the enemy could not get hold of it in April 1918. The town had to suffer from the long-range artillery fire and from aeroplane bombs.

The Cathedral of Amiens, which, like that of Reims, is a jewel of Gothic art, has fortunately suffered little from the enemy bombardment, thanks to the precautions taken by us.

HANGARD-EN-SANTERRE was the scene of extremely bloody struggles; it was here that the liaison between the French and the British armies had been established. The Germans tried to sever them, but British and French co-operated skilfully in defence, so that Von Hutier's army suffered heavy losses without obtaining any result.

MOREUIL was taken by the Germans on April 3, who, attacking in great numbers our weak cavalry skirmishers, succeeded in crossing the Avre and scaling the heights to the west; they advanced as far as

K 2

Merville. Next morning the brilliant counter-attack of a fresh division, hastily brought up, threw them back on the Anchin farm and the wood of Arrière-Court.

GRIVESNES AND LE PLESSIER-GRIVESNES were the scenes of stubborn fighting. In the large park of Grivesnes castle a colonel, with his company and a few machine-guns, though already encircled, defended himself bravely ; a few staff-officers attended to the machine-

Ph. Léry

AMIENS.   The Cathedral

guns, and an intelligence officer operated a Hotchkiss.   Their heroism was rewarded : they were delivered by a reserve battalion, Grivesnes and Plessier-Grivesnes remained with us.   We had to abandon them a few days later before violent attacks.   The village was retaken at the end of July, just before the great offensive of August 8, and our troops progressed far enough eastward of Grivesnes.   One thousand five hundred prisoners remained in our hands.

Sector 12—Picardy

MONTDIDIER was taken by the Germans on March 27, 1918, one of the most critical days for the Allies' destiny. In spite of their efforts the Germans could not succeed in advancing west of Montdidier, a firm resistance was in front of them. They attempted to attack to the North of Ailly-sur-Noye, but to no purpose.

Montdidier was retaken by the troops of General Debeney on August 10. The town, almost entirely encircled, was evacuated by the enemy ; it had been destroyed by the fire and the bombardment of our artillery. We crossed the Avre a little to the north of the town on a footbridge, twenty times destroyed, and as often rebuilt by our Engineers.

THE REGION OF THE MATZ was the witness in the beginning of June of a violent German attack with Compiègne for an objective. On June 9 the enemy, with 170,000 men, attacked our line passing through Montdidier, Lassigny, Noyon Nampcel. He succeeded in progressing

Ph. Lécu

SAINT-QUENTIN. La Basilique.

to a depth of about 7 miles, but on the 11th General Mangin counter-attacked him on his right and succeeded in pushing him back towards Ressons-sur-Matz. Some squadrons of aeroplanes gave valuable help in this counter-attack by bombing the German battalions in full daylight.

HAM which the Germans had occupied since 1914, was evacuated by them at the time of their retreat of March 1917. They got hold of it again during their advance of 1918. General Debeney's army eventually secured possession in September 1918.

The Germans blew up the principal buildings of Ham, including the castle where Prince Louis Napoléon, afterwards Napoléon III, was imprisoned, and from whence he succeeded in escaping.

NESLES has undergone nearly the same fate as Ham. At the time of their retreat of 1917 the Germans were about to set it on fire, but were prevented from doing so by the rapid advance of our troops.

SAINT-QUENTIN had to suffer a great deal from German occupation. Our troops could not take the town in 1917. At the time of the great offensive of 1918), our troops constantly Quentin. Fierce struggles the banks of the Crozat taken at the end of September pation we were compelled heavy damage resulted. comparison with the syste-looting organised by the Debeney's army (August 8, attempted to capture Saint-took place, particularly on Canal. Saint-Quentin was ber, 1918. During its occu-to fire at the town, and But this was nothing in matic destruction and Germans.

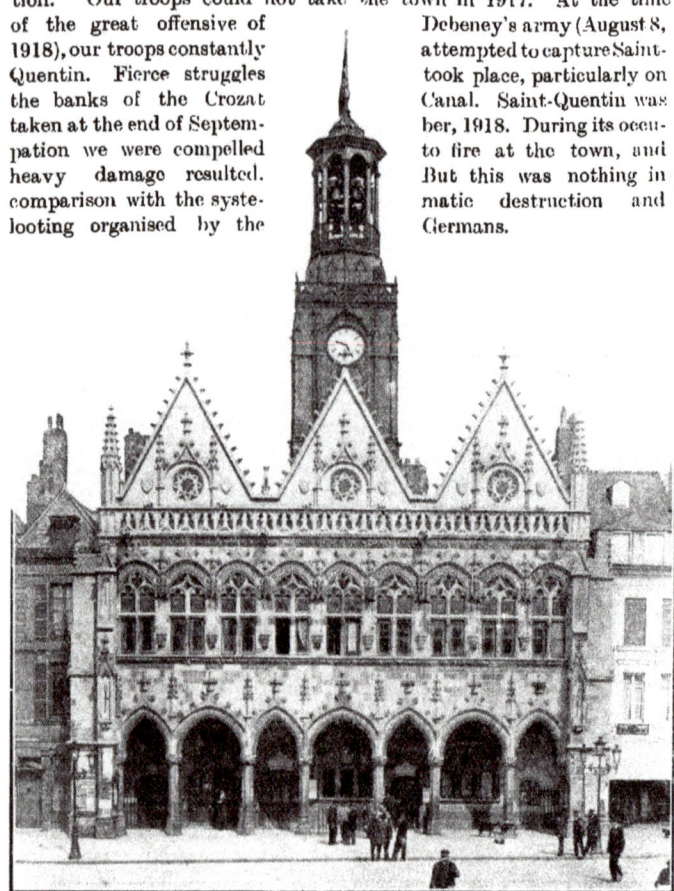

P. Lévy

SAINT-QUENTIN. Hôtel-de-Ville.

MOY and **TERGNIER** were the theatres of furious battles at the time of our advance of March 1917 and August 1918, when the Germans desired to secure their retreat on the famous Hindenburg line.

Sector 12—Picardy

LA FÈRE, which we hoped to capture in April 1917, was so well defended naturally by the surrounding marshes that we could not take it. Even in 1918, the town fell into our hands only because it was threatened with encirclement.

NOYON was the frontier town nearest to Paris, and a sentence often repeated in the papers and in the Chamber to recall the presence of the enemy was: "The Germans are at Noyon." Noyon was abandoned by the invader in his retreat of March 1917, after violent rearguard fighting. At the time of our offensive of 1918 Noyon fell into our hands on September 3. After the German retreat of 1917 the damages were not relatively considerable, but, on the contrary, in 1918 the artillery fire and the systematic destruction by the Germans seriously injured this previously prosperous little town.

The line **CARLEPONT,** Tracy-le-Mont, Tracy-le-Val, Moulin-sous-Touvent, **AUTRECHES,** Saint-Christophe and Nouvron constituted the front line till March 1917. In the church of Tracy-le-Val the Germans unsealed the tomb of the Laigle family, and examined the coffins for jewels to confiscate. The plateau overlooking Moulin-sous-Touvent and the plateau of Nouvron were in 1915 the scenes of violent struggles, and all this sector was agitated till the retreat of the Germans.

This line was also the starting-point of the counter-offensive of General Mangin on August 20, 1918. On the very first day we took 8,000 prisoners and progressed about 7 miles.

RETHONDES.—It was at the station of Rethondes that General Foch's special train was resting when armistice was asked for by the German envoys.

COMPIÈGNE.—The Germans only passed through Compiègne in 1914, and the charming little town had been spared. The French G.H.Q., after the German retreat of March 1917, fixed its quarters here, but had to leave at the time of the spring offensive 1918. Compiègne was the object of the attack on the Matz on June 9; the town was submitted to a very violent fire of the long-range gun, and suffered very much, especially from aeroplane shelling, which did not omit even the hospital.

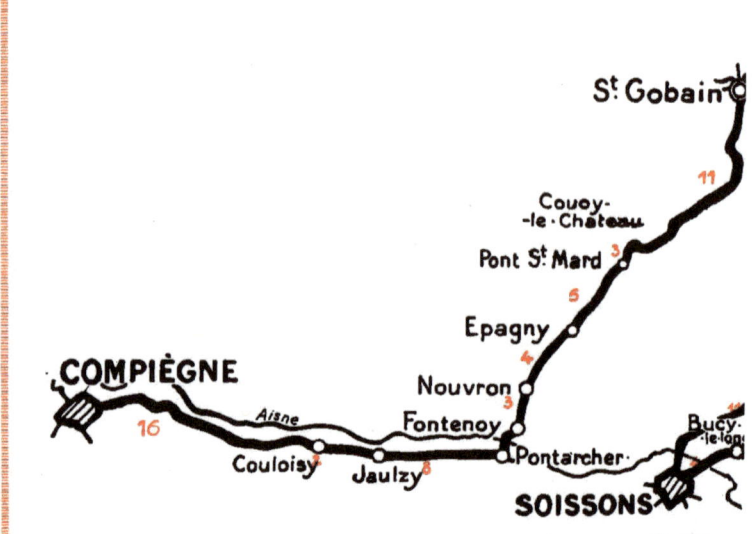

Sector 13

Chemin des Dames

Route

The tourist may start either from *Compiègne*, when coming from *Paris*, or from *Château-Thierry*, if coming from *Reims*. In the latter case, he will take the contrary route to that shown beneath.

From Compiègne, follow the road south of the Aisne through *Couloisy, Jaulzy* up to *Pontarcher*; there cross the Aisne and go up through *Fontenoy* and *Nouvron*. From Nouvron, continue straight on to *Epagny*,

Sector 13—Chemin des Dames

Pont-Saint-Mard, visit *Coucy-le-Château*, then retake the road of *Saint-Gobain*; visit Saint-Gobain and the mirror factory, then go to *Laon* through *Cessières*. From Laon, go north to *Crépy-en-Laonnois* and visit on the *Mont-de-Joie* the emplacements of the long-range guns ("Big Berthas") which bombarded Paris at the end of 1918.

Come back to Laon and take the road of *Anizy-le-Château* through *Chaillevois*; at Anizy, turn to the left, see *Pinon*, then go straight to the left to *Chavignon*; at Chavignon, turn to the right. At 1,500 ft. on the left of the road, observe the *Fort de la Malmaison*. Then take again the road to the *Moulin de Laffaux*. From the Mill of Laffaux, descend on *Soissons*, visit Soissons, then take the road north of the Aisne, visit *Bucy-le-Long, Celles-sur-Aisne* and the fort; finally *Vailly*. If, at the time the tourist arrives at these places, the Chemin des Dames should be practicable, he should continue straight on past Vailly, stopping now and again to scale the heights to his right, from which he will be able to overlook the whole battlefield. He should pass to *Beaurieux*, then to *Pontavert*, there he should turn to the left and go to *Craonelle*, and from thence, turning to the right, to *Craonne* and *Corbeny*. At Corbeny turn to the right, and follow the road from Laon to Reims to about 2 miles past *Berry-au-Bac*. Then turn to the right through *Cormicy*. At *Roucy*, turn to the left and reach *Fismes* through *Ventelay* and *Romain*. Visit Fismes; then take the road of Soissons, turn to the left at *Bazoches*, see *Mont-Notre-Dame* and reach *Rozières* through *Branges and Nampteuil*.

From Rozières go down to *Buzancy, Villemontoire* and *Hartennes*. On issuing from Hartennes, turn to the left and reach *Vierzy*.

At Vierzy continue south to *Longpont* and reach *Villers-Cotterets*.

From Villers-Cotterets, go down to *Ferté Milon*, there turn to the left and reach *Fère-en-Tardenois*, through *Troesnes*, an extreme point of the German advance, and *Oulchy-le-Château*.

From Fère-en-Tardenois, reach again the road north of the Marne, and gain *Château-Thierry* through *Jaulgonne* and *Mont-Saint-Père*.

As an alternative, turn to the left on arriving at the Marne, visit *Dormans* and come back to Château-Thierry through the road south of the Marne. From Château-Thierry, one must not fail to visit the wood of *Belleau*, immortalised by the bravery of the American Marines.

HOTELS

CHATEAU-THIERRY

HOTEL DU CYGNE.
    5 and 7 Rue des Filoirs.
    Telephone.
           25 rooms. Central heating.
           Garage 12.

HOTEL RESTAURANT JEAN DE LA FONTAINE.
    54 Grande-Rue.
           Modern comfort. Tea room.
           Garage 10.

HOTEL DE LA GARE.

Sector 13—Chemin des Dames

FISMES

GRAND HOTEL DE L'ECU and HOTEL DE LA HURE.

Owner : A. Delrue.
Telephone.

Terrace and rooms with splendid view of the valley. A.C.F. Silver medal of the T.C.F. Baths. Garage.

HOTEL DU NORD ET D'ANGLETERRE.

Place de la Gare.
Owner : P. Maurey.

Silver Medal of the T.C.F. This Hotel, having been destroyed by the bombardments, has been luxuriously re-established in another building.

SOISSONS

HOTEL DU LA CROIX D'OR.
Telephone 109.

50 Rooms. Electric lighting. Centre of town. Modern comfort. Garage 20.

VILLERS-COTTERETS

HOTEL DE LA CHASSE.
Telephone 62.

Modern comfort.

Historical Account

The region in which the two battles of the Chemin des Dames were delivered has no individual historical associations. It is divided between the three provinces of Champagne, Picardy, and the Island of France. At the Revolution it was almost entirely included in the district of Aisne. It underwent the invasions of 1814 and 1815. A violent battle was sustained by Napoleon I at Craonne and another at Château-Thierry.

Economic Account

From the agricultural point of view the Aisne is a very rich region. This prosperity is the result, however, of stubborn work for the improvement of the soil.

At present they cultivate corn and beetroot. Breeding (horses and oxen) is carried on extensively. The textile industry is here very highly developed. There are also sugar factories. Note once more the famous mirror factory of Saint Gobain.

Sector 13—Chemin des Dames

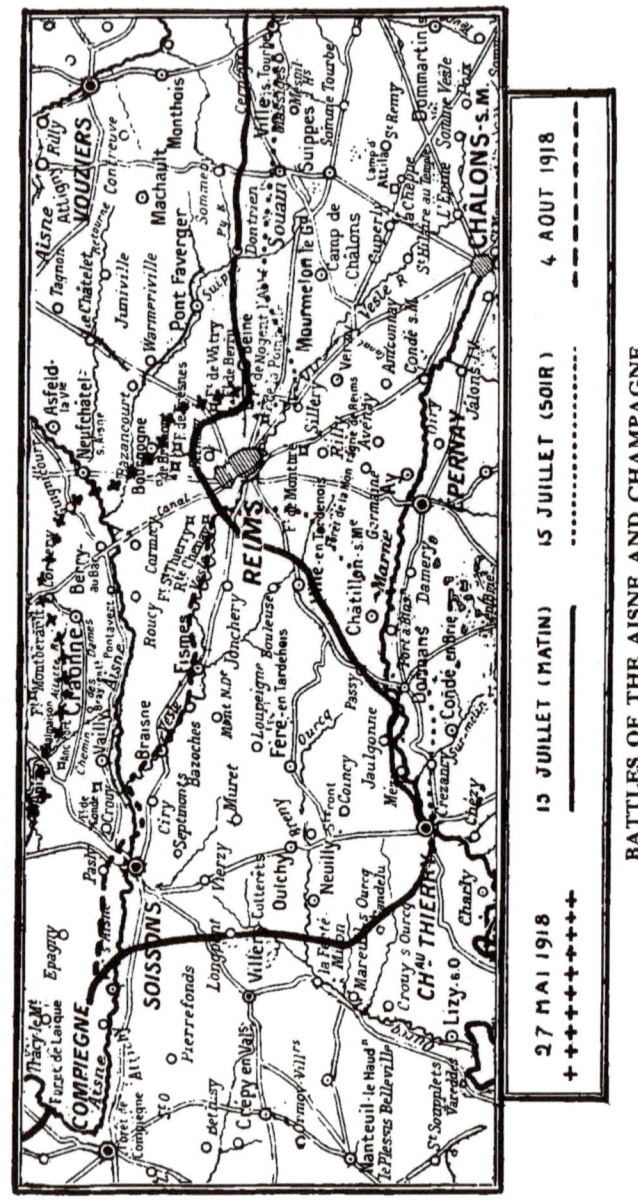

BATTLES OF THE AISNE AND CHAMPAGNE

Ph. Rol

Gen. MANGIN

Ph. P. Petit

Gen. FAYOLLE

Ph. Meley

Gen. DESGOUTTE

C. Sect. Ph. Armée

Gen. BERTHELOT

Short Account of the Operations

The Chemin des Dames takes equal place with the Yser and Verdun as one of the most glorious battlefields of France, and it ranks also among those which witnessed the noblest examples of French heroism. After their defeat on the Marne, the Germans had withdrawn to the ridges overlooking the north bank of the Aisne. In the Spring of 1917 we undertook a great offensive drive in this region; a gigantic attack was conceived. But Hindenburg, having foreseen the operation, had massed on the plateau of Chemin des Dames and on the massif of Moronvilliers 400,000 men. On April 16 our troops commenced the attack west of Reims. We succeeded, in the face of enormous difficulties, in scaling the ridges which overhang the Aisne. Our artillery preparation had been violent, but the enemy had dug in the chalk vast underground caverns 30 and 60 feet deep, which could not be reached by our shells. On the 17th our attack extended east of Reims, and our troops, progressing from two to three miles, captured a part of the hill region. From April 16 to 29, on the Craonne and Moronvilliers plateaux, we made altogether 23,000 prisoners and took 175 guns. Bitter enemy counter-attacks failed. Craonne was taken on the 4th, the Chemin des Dames on the 5th. The battle then became, as at Verdun, a series of extremely obstinate local combats, and throughout June and July many fierce counter-attacks were beaten off. On October 23 a strong attack brought us (almost without any losses) to the Fort of Malmaison, and compelled the Germans to retire on the borders of the Ailette.

The Chemin des Dames, which we had acquired and kept at the price of so much blood, was lost within a few hours at the time of the German formidable attack of May 27, 1918. When this sector was very calm and guarded by very few troops, the Germans were preparing secretly a large offensive with the object of cutting the French armies in two. After a terrific bombardment with gas shells, the enemy attacked. Our troops, completely surprised, could not hold out before such numbers; they withdrew to the Marne. The Germans took Château-Thierry and Dormans. Nevertheless, they were once more stopped, and soon the second Marne victory began. On July 18 General Mangin attacked the salient of Château-Thierry. He had well concealed his plans of attack ; a storm prevented the enemy from observing the final preparations ; without the usual artillery preparation, and only preceded by a formidable moving barrage, our infantry stormed to the assault at 4.30 in the morning. The Germans were even more surprised than we were on May 27. They abandoned their guns and machine guns, and either took to flight or surrendered. General Desgoutte attacked on the 19th south of the Marne, and succeeded in crossing the river. Château-Thierry was taken on July 26 by the able participation of an infantry and marine division of the American army. Ludendorff ordered a retreat, and the German troops retired on the Aisne and the Vesle, almost as far as our positions of 1915. In our offensive of August 20 the Chemin des Dames was taken in reverse by Mangin's army attacking from the west, and our troops soon reconquered the famous Roman road. On August 6 Foch received his Marshal's bâton with this citation : " Paris delivered, Soissons and Château-Thierry reconquered after heavy fighting, 200 villages delivered, 35,000 prisoners, 700 guns captured, the confidently proclaimed hopes of the enemy destroyed, the glorious Allied armies thrown in one victorious bound from the Marne banks to the banks of the Aisne ; here are the results of a manœuvre as admirably conceived by the High Command as executed by our incomparable Generals."

War Facts

COUCY-LE-CHATEAU.—On March 20, 1917, our troops pursuing the retiring enemy arrived at Coucy. They had to cross the canal and five branches of the river under a constant fire of gas shells. Seven whole days they had to fight in the rain and snow. On the 25th a German counter-attack made a great effort, but failed. On the 26th our soldiers slipped through the marshes at the foot of the Mount Coucy ; they attempted and almost succeeded in encircling the position. The Germans, perceiving the inevitable results of the manœuvre, surrendered or escaped. They had already accomplished their Vandal works, however, before the arrival of the French. The Castle of Coucy was quite in ruins. It had been one of the most beautiful buildings since the feudal period. The motto of the lord was " I am neither King, nor Duke, nor Count, I am the Lord of Coucy."

The castle contained an enormous dungeon (the biggest in France) about 160 feet. This dungeon had a diameter of 93 feet, and comprised

Sector 13—Chemin des Dames

three overlying vaults. Four enormous towers rose at the angles of the castle. The surrounding walls were 21 by 30 feet deep, and the Germans expended 30,000 kilos of explosive in order to reduce this splendid monument to ruins.

SAINT-GOBAIN is famous the world over for its mirror factory, a visit to which is extremely interesting. South-east of Saint-Gobain extends the forest. It was in this forest that were placed the famous long-range guns which on March 23, 1918, began to shell Paris. These guns were installed on the spur of the Mont-de-Joie, north-west of Crépy-en-Laonnais, not far from the road La-Fère-Laon.

LAON was the object of our attack of April 16, 1917, on the Chemin des Dames, but it could not be reached. It was only on October 12 1918, that our troops entered the town.

Ph. L'cg

COUCY-LE-CHATEAU.

PINON.—At the time of the German advance of May 27, 1918, on the Chemin des Dames, three French battalions occupied the forest of Pinon. They held out there for more than 24 hours with a courage above all praise, and eventually a pigeon carried off this despatch : " The three last men of the three last battalions have just surrendered." The sacrifice of this fine regiment was not useless, the enemy could not extend the attack westward in spite of his repeated efforts.

THE FORT OF MALMAISON has remained famous through the French offensive of October 23 to 26, 1917, which is always known as the victory of Malmaison. The artillery preparation, minutely arranged, was extremely violent, and lasted six days and six nights. The Germans were thus fully notified, they had massed on the fort 100,000 men with the order to hold to death ; their force was but slightly less than ours. The attack was launched on the 23rd, on a

159

bitterly cold morning. The battle lasted four days, but on the 26th, at evening, the desired objective was more than attained. On a front of 8 miles we had made a progress of 4 miles' depth ; 11,000 prisoners remained in our hands with 180 guns.

THE MILL OF LAFFAUX was a witness of epic struggles. It was attacked on May 5, 1917, by a division of dismounted cuirassiers. As the mill overlooked an important position, strongly organised, progress was only accomplished at a heavy cost in men. The cuirassiers were, however, assisted by a group of tanks. At noon the mill was taken, and even passed, but our troops finally had to retire to the line of the mill, which remained in our hands. Numerous and violent German counter-attacks failed. The Mill of Laffaux was lost at the end of May 1918, and re-conquered during the advance of General Mangin, at the moment when, having converged towards east, he took the Chemin des Dames in reverse.

Ph. Lévy

SOISSONS.—The Cathedral.

SOISSONS, re-taken by us after the Marne victory, fell into the hands of the Germans at the time of their offensive of May 27, 1918. Soissons received in the very day of the attack 1,200 shells and the town was set on fire by the bombardments. The Brandenburgers succeeded in getting hold of it after murderous street fighting. At the time of the French offensive of April 1917, Soissons had been released, and it was thought that the town would no longer have to suffer from the enemy bombardments. It was not so, and the bombardment of 1918 surpassed all previous efforts of destruction in its ferocity and inhumanity.

THE FORT OF CONDÉ marked, before our attack, the extremity of a point of the German line usually called the Salient of Vailly. The reduction of this salient, commenced on April 16, was consummated within five days, our line then passing through Laffaux, Sancy, Jouy and the slopes of Chemin des Dames. At the time of the German offensive of May, 1918, our troops defended themselves bravely at the Fort of Condé. The artillerymen firing point-blank at 300 feet shelled the German masses with fearful precision.

THE CHEMIN DES DAMES is an old Roman road following the hill ridge which lines the right bank of the Aisne. It fell into our hands on May 5, 1917, with 5,000 prisoners. On the 6th the Germans launched two violent counter-attacks, which failed completely. These counter-attacks were renewed later with increasing persistence Hurtebise was particularly attacked in the beginning of June by the Crown Prince's troops, who sustained a bloody failure.

The Chemin des Dames, with certain corners of Verdun, was one of the most murderous points of the front. Asphyxiating gases, aerial torpedoes, shells, grenades, mines, all means were employed from either side in order to force the adversary to submission. This ground, so dearly conquered and so dearly defended, was lost on May 27, 1918. Our troops, inferior in numbers, and surprised by the weight of the artillery fire and the enormous infantry masses, could not hold out. General Mangin recaptured the Chemin des Dames in September, 1918, but this time the plateau was reached by a flanking movement.

THE CAVERN OF THE DRAGON was an underground German shelter dug in the quarry of the Chemin des Dames, north-west of Hurtebise. It comprised quite a system of superimposed galleries in which a thousand men could find shelter. Our shells could not reach this impenetrable vault, but succeeded in obstructing two of the entrances and our troops launched to the attack could hardly find the third, blocked up as it was by German dead. The interior of the cavern was littered with corpses.

CRAONNE was taken by us on May 4, 1917, when, after a scientific artillery preparation, an infantry division attacked the whole spur of Craonne. Three companies within ten minutes got hold of the village, seizing 225 prisoners. What was left of the assault line conquered all the accesses. The Germans instantly attempted to retake this invaluable observation post. They counter-attacked violently in the nights of the 5th and 6th, but in vain. From July 19 to 24, the Crown Prince continually attempted to recapture Craonne. On the 19th he launched, on the east side of the Chemin des Dames, three fresh divisions of Brandenburgers and a Guards division ; the Germans made some temporary progress on the plateau, but by night they were back at their starting positions. On the 21st, after a tremendous artillery preparation, the enemy again assaulted, but in spite of his efforts he could not advance. On the 24th a return offensive from our side gave us back almost all the lost ground.

At Mont-Notre-Dame there was a large French hospital, and the German advance was so rapid that it could not be evacuated. The enemy took it and carefully tended the numerous wounded. At Mont-Notre-Dame, as at Fismes, there were depots of motor-lorries.

They captured these also, a very valuable prize, as they had been very short of tyres and inner tubes, and found there an enormous stock of pneumatics.

VIERZY-BUZANCY.—Buzancy, which constituted for the enemy an important position, was taken on July 30 by the 15th (Scotch) division, whom Mangin had eulogised as " splendid troops " ; the victory of Buzancy was the deliverance of Soissons.

OULCHY-LE-CHÂTEAU and **OULCHY-LA-VILLE** offered a long resistance to the advance of Mangin's army at the end of July, 1918, but our troops were able to manœuvre skilfully and progressed on the hills south of the Ourcq. Finally the bastion of the plateau of Hartennes, threatened with envelopment, gave way.

FÈRE-EN-TARDENOIS.—The enemy attacked Fère-en-Tardenois on May 29, 1918. A French division in charge of the defence held its ground sixteen hours, assisted by the machine guns and French aeroplanes. During the night the Germans received reinforcements, and the next morning, the 30th, at dawn we had to give way ; at 7 o'clock in the morning a counter attack gave us back Fère, yet at nine o'clock once more we had to retire. At the time of our counter-offensives violent struggles took place from the 28th to the 31st around Fère. The Americans, fighting by our side, covered themselves with glory. Fère was occupied, and soon afterwards the Germans began the retreat on the Aisne and the Vesle.

CHÂTEAU-THIERRY was the extreme point of the German advance in 1918 ; the town was occupied on May 31st. The Germans did not attempt then to cross the Marne, as they concentrated on Villers-Cotterets. At the time of the attack of July 15, however, the Germans crossed the Marne near Château-Thierry, but could progress no further, especially on the west. Château-Thierry was retaken by the French troops on July 21 ; on the 20th, at evening, the few hundreds of inhabitants who had remained in the town were shut up in the church of Saint Crespin ; on the 21st, at morning, not seeing any Germans, they decided to attempt to go out, and were much surprised at finding a French soldier on the square ; they threw themselves on him and carried him off in triumph.

||||||||||||||||||||||||||||||||||||||||||||||||||||||||||||||||||||||||||||||||||||||||||||||||||||||||||||||||||||

The Americans
in the Château-Thierry Sector

It was in the region of Château-Thierry that American troops for the first time joined in a modern battle.

They were ordered at the end of May 1918 to arrest the German push on the Marne between Verneuil and Château-Thierry. Von Boehm could not cross the river. The wood of Belleau, north-west of Château-Thierry, is famous all over America ; there the second American Marine infantry division covered itself with glory. On June 25, 1918, at evening, after a terrible battle, the Belleau wood was taken.

Gen. PERSHING

On July 1, the village of Vaux was taken and 500 prisoners seized. On July 18, the Americans were attacking amidst our enthusiastic soldiers. Having thrown away their coats, they ran against the enemy with a splendid ardour. Torcy was taken by them within five minutes. The village of Belleau, then that of Civry, fell into their hands, the losses having been light, and progress swift.

On July 31 the enemy resisted near Fère-en-Tardenois, and heavy struggles took place. The Americans of the Dégoutte army triumphed there over two divisions of the Guards. Sergy was taken and retaken four times. Seringue, lost after two days' occupation, was retaken by the troops from Ohio.

Fismes was the scene of terrible fighting. The Banks of the Vesle were the witnesses of the most glorious traits of heroism of the gallant American troops. It was there, perhaps, that most of our heroic Allies fell. All the determined efforts attempted for the occupation of Fismes were useless. The Germans enjoyed a very favourable position where they had massed their best troops.

On August 28, 1918, General Pershing issued an inspiring message of congratulations to the 1st and 3rd American Corps, which had distinguished themselves in the sector between the Marne and the Vesle : " In this moment of the war," he said, " you have shown that the spirit of initiative and the energy of the Americans can be applied to the trials of war as well as to works of peace."

Sector 14—Somme

Route

From *Amiens* visit *Villers Bretonneux*, then return to Amiens. Then go to *Albert* and see *Pozières, Mametz Wood, Thiepval, Beaumont-Hamel,* then on to *Bapaume* and *Combles.*

HOTELS.

AMIENS

HOTEL DE L'UNIVERS.

ST. QUENTIN

HOTEL DE FRANCE ET L'ANGLETERRE.

> NOTE.—The normal charges are as follows :—
> Breakfast from fr. 3 to 3.50. Lunch or Dinner from fr. 10 to 20. Bedroom from fr. 10 to 18. The average cost per day is 40 francs, but during July and August it is advisable to reckon this as 50 francs. There is a tax of 10 per cent. on all first-class hotel bills.

Historical Account

This part of the country changed hands several times between the 15th and the 18th centuries. It was part of a French province in the 15th century, but both the Dutch and the Spanish challenged the French possession successfully. In the 18th century, however, the French won the district back, and it has remained in their hands ever since. It is interesting to note that Villers Brettoneux was the scene of the first battle between the Prussians and the French Army of the North on November 27, 1870.

Economic Account

This Department is one of the best cultivated in France. Beetroot is a staple crop, especially in the Peronne district. Cereals are grown throughout the department, and the breeding of horses and cattle is also carried on extensively. Market gardening and peat cutting are favourite activities of the peasants in the neighbourhood of Amiens and Abbeville. Phosphate of lime is quite an important mineral product. The following industries are well established and give employment to a large number of the people :—Velvet, hosiery, linen, hemp, flour-milling, paper making, brewing, dyeing, saw-milling, iron founding and forging.

Short Account of the Operations

The valley of the Somme and the district to the north has been during the whole war one of the most constant fields of carnage and heroism. It would be impossible to discover a sector, with the possible exception of Ypres, which has had the privilege of illustrating in such a high degree the spirit of courage, determination and self-sacrifice with which the British troops are imbued. This sector has witnessed two of the most unique battles of modern warfare. In the advance of 1916 and the withdrawal of 1918, we have thrust upon us examples of heroism, tenacity and daring such as can never be surpassed on the Western or any other front.

In July 1916, when the Great Anglo-French offensive to relieve Verdun was inaugurated, the Allies had only just attained a temporary equality with the enemy in man-power and heavy guns. The effects of this levelling-up were immediately visible in the fierce and bloody conflicts which followed. For the first time the Germans felt the devastating results of a sustained shell-fire, accurately directed and ruthlessly employed. Our advance was steady and certain. In the first four days our troops swept over the enemy's strongest system of defence, which he had done his utmost to render impregnable. In a few places isolated redoubts and fortified villages still held out, but by a succession of daring rushes, these also were eventually captured. Round the villages of Thiepval, Ovillers, Contalmaison, and Beaumont-Hamel, the resistance was obstinate and severe, and many bitter counter-attacks were delivered by the enemy. Mametz wood was only secured after three days' terrible fighting, frequently hand-to-hand combats were in progress, and the losses on either side were heavy. These scattered remnants of former forests continually gave great trouble to our men in an attack, and constituted a formidable rallying point for the enemy's counter-attacks. During the next four months a steady deterioration took place in the morale of the German forces, in some measure due to the now constant weakness of their artillery support, and our forward movement became consequently accelerated. To counteract this process of attrition, the German authorities, in the latter half of the year, resorted to a policy of systematic destruction of all roads, trees, bridges and other means of communication and observation in the rear of their lines, previous to a withdrawal. This procedure, inhuman and relentless though it was, did have a considerable influence on our subsequent operations. Much valuable time had necessarily to be spent after each periodical occupation, in repairing the ravages, connecting the bridges, and reconstructing means of supply. In this way the complete culmination of our success was indefinitely hampered.

Notwithstanding these difficulties, by the end of the year most important and strategic positions had been gained, and 38,000 prisoners,

165

as well as many guns, captured. In addition, the heavy pressure previously exercised on Verdun was practically removed, and the fighting strength and efficiency of the German forces was notably worn down. In March 1917 the enemy had, however, decisively entrenched himself in a new system, henceforward known as the Hindenburg line.

In March 1918, the Great German reaction against this blow was commenced, taking the form of a supreme attempt to so shatter the British line at its junction with the French that a dissolution would be imposed and the path to final victory opened. With an unparalleled concentration of troops and artillery, only made possible by the defection of our Eastern Ally, they delivered a series of overwhelming attacks on various portions of our new front on the Somme. Assisted as they were by a concatenation of events, far-reaching in their calamitous import, an enormous success was compassed, and the thin lines of the British were compelled to undertake a fighting retreat, regretfully relinquishing to the sacrilegious touch of the enemy, the venerated hills and villages of their former glory. By this hard, but necessary, expedient, a break was avoided, and liaison between all the armies maintained in its integrity. The conduct of the British in this withdrawal fulfilled the noblest traditions of their race, and it was in no small measure, owing to their skill, self-sacrifice and obstinacy in defence, that the Allied forces were eventually enabled to reorganise and consolidate in time to effectually prevent the spasmodic advance of the enemy achieving their merely secondary objective—the capture of Amiens.

Just east of that town, the final stand of our armies took place, and from thence their stubborn units could not be dislodged by all exertions of the foe. In the course of the retreat they had inflicted heavy losses upon the reckless and confident enemy legions, and in most cases their remarkable endurance had permitted the guns and staff personnel to be withdrawn safely. Many regiments arrived at the bases completely exhausted by lack of sleep and constant fighting. Some had had no sleep for forty-eight hours, and their physical condition was so attenuated as to allow them to snatch their minutes of slumber whilst still on the march.

On March 26 the Governments of France and Great Britain deemed it advisable to appoint Marshal Foch Generalissimo of the Allied Armies, with supreme control of the operations. The immediate effect of this long-felt want of proper co-ordination was directly evident, for on July 20 it was found possible to once more regain the offensive, and the enemy, exhausted by his stupendous losses and disheartened by the failure of his strategic plan, was slowly driven back. The lost ground was quickly re-occupied, a general movement ensued along the whole front, and the forces of right began their triumphant progress which ended on November 11 with Victory and Peace. This valley of the Somme will be regarded by posterity as the decisive theatre in which was determined the issue of the Great War.

||||||||||||||||||||||||||||||||||||||||||||||||||||||||||||||||||||||||||||||||||||||||||||||||||||||||||||||||||||||||||||||||

War Facts

POZIÈRES.—This small village was the scene of the most terrible combats during the 1916 offensive, when the first Australian division were entrusted with the task of carrying its fortified defences. The principal contested point was the cemetery, which lies a little to the west of the main Albert-Bapaume road, and which was not secured without heavy losses. The German troops garrisoning this stronghold were of the Prussian Guards, and they put up a desperate resistance. However, on July 25 the last elements in enemy possession were captured. In the German sweep of 1918 no fighting of any importance took place here, and in our final advance to victory it was occupied in one rush.

THIEPVAL.—Another great centre of opposition in the first battle of the Somme ; the continued counter-attacks which were launched by the enemy from and around this village, succeeded in holding up its capture for many months. On the spur to the north of the village there was a strongly entrenched work known as Liepzig salient, which was only taken after a bloody combat, and after its almost total destruction by shell fire. It was not until September 26 that the position was entirely in our hands. The capture was rendered extremely difficult by reason of the adjoining fortresses, which made any serious attempt at encirclement costly. These places were called Zollen Redoubt, Schwaben Redoubt, and Stuff Redoubt, and were eventually carried by a frontal attack. Thiepval shared the fate of all the Somme villages in 1918, and also participated in the subsequent rescue by the Allies.

VILLERS BRETONNEUX.—One of the last successes gained by the Germans in their 1918 offensive was a temporary capture of this village, which constituted at that time one of the most important bulwarks of our rapidly stabilising lines. Orders were issued by the General commanding the 4th and 5th Australian divisions for its recapture the same night, and at 10 o'clock his troops advanced to the assault. A night operation of this character, undertaken at such short notice, was an enterprise of incomparable daring. There was no artillery preparation, the troops had no knowledge of the ground they had to traverse, and it may without hesitation be placed as one of the most hazardous expeditions of the war. Fighting took place throughout the night in the environs of the village, and daybreak found the gallant Colonials well into the centre of Villers ; additional troops were rushed up and by 4 p.m. they had entirely cleared the position. It was in the German attack on this village that the German tanks accomplished their first bit of creditable work, and were instrumental in bringing the objective within the reach of their infantry. Although they were found to be much slower in manœuvre than our own representatives, they were heavily armed and caused many casualties when in a favourable situation.

BAPAUME.—This important town, whose strategic uses as a road and railway centre were innumerable, remained beyond the reach of our operations in 1916 ; but in the final allied advance in August it became one of the principal objectives and was evacuated by the enemy in the early morning of August 28. The New Zealand division took possession and were never disturbed, though many fierce counter-attacks were sustained.

BEAUMONT-HAMEL.—This stronghold resisted all attacks by us in the first battle of the Somme until November 11, when it was carried in an overwhelming rush. It stands on the west of the crest of a spur, whose elevation, though only 350 feet, gave it a dominating position over the low lying land adjacent.

ALBERT.—This town was entered by the Germans in their great 1918 offensive on March 26, but owing to the murderous fire of the British they were utterly unable to debouch on the other side. They had also to endure constant shelling at short range by two brigades of field artillery, and for some time desultory fighting by the opposing infantry took place in the outskirts. For two days the weight of fire compelled the enemy to remain passive, but during the whole of the time he was receiving constant accretions of men and guns, and on March 28 four separate efforts were made to issue from their death-trap. Three of these attacks were smashed by the guns, but the fourth by sheer velocity broke through the line, and once more the affair was in a state of flux. A successful attempt was made, however, to stabilise the fronts, and about 2 miles west of Albert, our line was temporarily established. The town, unfortunately, afforded the Germans splendid cover for assembling troops and massing an attack, and on April 4 another convulsive heave was made in the direction of Amiens. The main attack fell on the Australians, and, though their conduct was most spirited, the enemy, by dint of a complete disregard for material losses, gained an additional foothold on the ridge. Turning their attention to the adjoining troops, they then pressed heavily on the Londoners, but despite their efforts in this direction, and probably because of the considerable depletion caused by the accurate fire of the Colonials, they were entirely unsuccessful. Albert was taken without trouble in our onset of August 21.

MAMETZ WOOD AND VILLAGE—Another hard nut which was cracked in the course of our first Somme offensive. Opposite Mametz part of our assembly trenches had been practically levelled by the enemy artillery, making it necessary for our infantry to advance to attack across 400 yards of open ground. None the less, they forced their way into Mametz, suffering fearful losses, and secured the defences on the opposing ridge.

COMBLES.—This village was captured by the Allied forces simultaneously on September 26, 1916. The British entering from the North, and the French from the South. No losses were encountered, as Combles had the day before been surrounded and menaced. A considerable tactical success was thus gained. Though lying in a hollow, the village was strongly fortified, and possessed, in addition to works which the enemy had constructed, exceptionally large cellars and galleries of a great depth underground, sufficient to give effectual shelter to many hundred troops and much material, against the heaviest bombardment. As was expected, great quantities of stores and ammunition were unearthed in these cellars after the occupation. In March 1918 the defence of Combles and its approaches was entrusted to the South African Division, which, in its magnificent resolve to stem the tide, and fulfil its duty, practically ceased to exist as a fighting unit. The commander, General Dawson, was wounded and taken prisoner while working a machine gun in Marrieres Wood, which lies on the slopes of the hill overlooking Combles to the East. His Brigade-Major was discovered dead at his side, and the majority of the survivors were seriously injured. This defence was spoken of by the enemy as one of the finest examples of courage in the whole war. After a desperate resistance in the streets, Combles was evacuated on March 24.

Sector 15—Cambrai

Route

Start at *Cambrai* and go slightly south-west to *Bourlon* and *Mœuvres*. Return to Cambrai, and take the road south to *Mesnières* and *Flesquières*.

HOTELS.

CAMBRAI

HOTEL DU MOUTON BLANC.

NOTE.—The normal charges are as follows :— Breakfast from fr. 3 to 3.50. Lunch or Dinner from fr. 10 to 20. Bedroom from fr. 10 to 18. The average cost per day is 40 francs, but during July and August it is advisable to reckon this as 50 francs. There is a tax of 10 per cent. on all first-class hotel bills.

Historical Account

The city and the surrounding country was, for many centuries, in the Middle Ages, continually passed from hand to hand between the Emperor Maximilian and the French King, until in 1678 it was finally incorporated with France.

Industrial Account

This area is largely concerned, in the manufacturing sense, with the production of beet sugar, of which there are many mills in the district. The tourist will notice that there is practically one per village. Cambrai itself, is, or was, mainly occupied with muslin and the weaving of other fine fabrics.

Short Account of the Operations

The great offensive which was to distinguish Cambrai as a battle centre in future remembrance, opened on the November 20, 1917, and extended over a front of 6 miles. The main reasons and aims of the attack have been described in detail in the general survey, and it will now suffice to reiterate that it was undertaken under pressure of external danger and with limited troops. To counterbalance in some measure this paucity of material force, an entirely novel method of

assault was employed. On the principal front of attack a large formation of tanks were deployed in the early morning on the 20th and it
was hoped that, by their inherent weight and power, the deep enemy
barbed wire entanglements would be broken up. This hope was realised,
and the main body of infantry, following close in their wake, speedily
captured the leading systems of the Hindenburg line. The Reserve
Line was also soon taken, and our troops commenced their final operations against the last defences of the town. Meanwhile, however,
a number of untoward incidents had combined to effect a serious delay
in our preconceived plans. In the attack on the village of Flesquières,
the resistance encountered was extremely obstinate, and very heavy
fighting took place. The enemy machine gunners completely commanded all approaches to the hill, and many attempts at assault met
with frightful losses. One example may serve to illustrate the nature of
the opposition. A German major of artillery, remaining alone at his
battery on the crest of the hill, served a gun single-handed, and knocked
out many of our tanks, before he was definitely located and killed.
The great bravery of this officer compelled the admiration of all ranks
of our army. Nevertheless, the village and its ridge were eventually
taken before the end of the day, but at some other vital points our
advance had been held up. At Mesnières, a village situated on the
Scheldt canal, parties of the enemy continued their bitter resistance
until a late hour in the afternoon. Ensconced in strongly built houses,
after having blown up the bridges to escape destruction by our
tanks, they were a source of constant anxiety to our men until they
were overcome. Their resistance, however, unfortunately gave time
for some hasty German reserves to be collected and thrown in to occupy
the village of Rumilly, one mile to the North, which we should otherwise have gained unopposed, and the time necessarily spent in these
and various other engagements was a most important item set against
our scheme. On other portions of the front the advance had been
much swifter, and in the centre our battalions at one period reached a
point only two miles outside the city itself. From henceforth the
Germans received daily reinforcements, and consequently the defence increased in stubborn obstinacy. Bourlon Wood, village and ridge, were
twice taken and retaken by the conflicting parties, but it was not found
possible in the end to hold the village with the force at our disposal,
and we withdrew to a stronger position in the wood. On November 22
Fontaine-Notre-Dame, the furthest point of our advance, was regained
by the enemy in the course of heavy fighting, and our reaction on the
following day, though supported by tanks and closely pressed, was
unable to secure permanent possession. Fresh German reinforcements
were now continually arriving, and every symptom of a determined
antagonism was exhibited. This rapidity of concentration obliged our
High Command to reconstruct entirely their original plans, and to
consider seriously the advisability of a relapse to temporary stabili-
sation as an alternative to the original idea of a great push. It
was determined that, in the circumstances, nothing could be effected,

offensively or defensively, without the capture of the Bourlon ridge. Another attempt was made, therefore, to storm the position, after a day spent in organisation, preparation and relief; and on the morning of the 23rd a final desperate effort was made to gain the coveted height and a similar attack was made contemporaneously with the object of rushing the village of Fontaine-Notre-Dame. The principal operation, after four hours' hard fighting, resulted in complete success. The whole of the ridge and the wood was captured, and Bourlon village, on the farther side, was entered. Hostile counter-attacks, however, persistently pressed, prevented us from consolidating our situation in Bourlon, and we eventually withdrew to our commanding position in the wood. Many attacks were delivered by the enemy in this region, but all were repulsed with heavy loss. The subsidiary push for Fontaine, although valiantly assisted by tanks, did not succeed in clearing the village, and at dusk we were forced to acknowledge failure in this direction. Nevertheless, many tanks remained in the streets long after nightfall, inflicting heavy loss on the Germans. Violent and bloody fighting took place in both these localities during the following days, each side striving to gain the advantage. Bourlon village was twice taken and retaken in hand-to-hand combats. On the second occasion, parties of the East Surrey Regiment hung on to the outskirts for two days until eventually relieved. Comparative quiet ensued until the end of November, when the great German reaction commenced. The formation of the country, which greatly facilitated the secret assembly of storm troops, and the weather conditions, which were misty, together with the special methods employed, all contributed to the success which was achieved. The surprise was complete, and almost before the men were fully conscious the swarms of the enemy were sweeping through our first lines. From then on, however, a bitter struggle was waged, and the breakage of our flank, which had at first seemed imminent, was averted by the constancy and heroism of the defenders. The guns, nearly overwhelmed in the first rush, were fought to the last, deeds of gallantry innumerable are recorded of the gunners, and the day, though unfortunate and disastrous, reflected nothing but credit on the British soldier. At one time the Germans had penetrated three miles behind our lines, but they were thrown back or destroyed, and a solid front was once more formed. In the North, at Bourlon and elsewhere, the offensive of Von Marwitz, though constantly repeated and supported by a violent artillery fire, was a failure, and even the renewed efforts to prosecute their advantage in the South came to nothing. The losses on either side in the course of the counter attacks were tremendous, and, by reason of their extraordinary reliance on mass effects, the enemy must have suffered by far the heavier. Many German battalions were seen to be entirely exterminated. The enemy, exhausted by the supreme concentration of his efforts, and the severity of his losses, was now reduced to a condition of temporary inaction, during which period it was decided that, in order to effectively conform to our new front in the South, our position around Bourlon and the vicinity should be readjusted. This withdrawal was accomplished without loss on the night of December 4. Regrettable as it was to give up to the enemy positions won at such a cost, and at the sacrifice of so many brave men, the necessity was imperative and the correct course obvious. Still, 11,000 prisoners and 150 guns were captured by us in our inaugural attack, and the extent to which our strategic aims were realised has been described in another portion of the book.

War Facts

FLESQUIÈRES.—This village was the vital point of the German defence. It was strongly organised, adequately garrisoned, and possessed natural advantages which are mainly accountable for the great difficulty experienced in the assault. The Château, which bears the name, stands on the summit of a small but dominating ridge, and was the centre of resistance. On the slopes of the hill, which constitutes the only direct method of approach, were countless nests of entrenched machine-guns, which assisted in making our advance arduous and destructive. In addition, the crest was protected by a high wall, behind which lay still more machine-guns, and behind them also a number of advanced field-guns. This strong point, defended with desperate bravery, held up our advancing troops for many hours, until circumspectly taken in flank and rear, when it became possible to overcome the defence.

MESNIÈRES.—lies on the eastern bank of the Scheldt, and from the very beginning of our Cambrai offensive was recognised as a point of strategic importance second only to Bourlon. The bridges at this place were the object of the first care of the assaulting Brigade, but the principal one had already been partially destroyed, and the attempted crossing of a leading tank brought about its collapse. This proved to be a serious misfortune, despite the discovery of a small footbridge lower down, for the delay caused by the event, coupled with the fierce fighting necessary to overcome the garrison, gave time for the Germans to occupy the more northerly village of Rumilly, and put up a better opposition than would otherwise have been likely. Subsequently, some picked battalions of the Prussian Guards delivered several counter-attacks, which invariably led to house-to-house combats. In the later stages of the operation, Mesnières was the scene of heroic struggles between the German Stormers and the 29th Division, who now held the salient. Though at one time cut off from both their adjoining units, they continued to hold their position with unconquerable valour and, notwithstanding all assaults, were never shaken. Field-Marshal Sir Douglas Haig afterwards sent a special order to General de Lisle, who was in command of the division, thanking him for his magnificent services.

173

BOURLON.—The name given to a wood, a ridge and a village, which respectively witnessed some of the most splendid qualities of determination and courage which have ever been exhibited to civilised man. This little trinity was the main object of contention for two weeks, during which time it was taken and retaken at least twice; finally, only the village remained impervious, some companies of the Yorkshire and Middlesex Regiments having entered the southern edge and dug themselves in among the ruined houses. The East Surreys, the Suffolks, and the Highland Light Infantry made constant attempts to gain the whole, but the enemy's strength was being augmented, and his attitude was resolute and even aggressive. Armour-piercing bullets were now being used by the Germans against our tanks, some-times with serious effect. On November 27, after a night of storm and a thick fall of snow, a further endeavour was made in this direction, but, after regaining portions of the devastated village, the brigades concerned were subjected to a searching fire and repeatedly counter-attacked, and it was not considered worth the heavy loss to hold the ground. In the end, we consolidated our position as far as possible in the wood, and on the ridge, and concentrated on an invulnerable defence in face of the German reaction which soon developed. In the sector of Mœuvres and Bourlon the violence of the German counter-attack was felt strongly, but all attacks were smashed by our artillery, who now at last enjoyed unexampled opportunities of displaying their efficiency. Wave upon wave of enemy infantry advanced in mass formation against our lines, only to be beaten to the earth by the overwhelming volume of our gun-fire. On the right flank, however, the Germans succeeded in entering the position, and they surrounded a company of the 13th Essex. After an anxious consultation the officers and non-commissioned officers of this gallant little body decided to fight to the last. During the night their firing could be heard, and when, in the morning, the trenches were recaptured, the whole band were found lying dead—true to their word.

MŒUVRES.—This village is situated on the western bank of the Canal du Nord, and was assigned as an objective to the extreme left wing of our army. It was protected on the left flank by a thick mass of gorse and trees known as Tadpole Copse. The copse was taken on November 22 by London and Irish (Ulster) troops, and the division engaged pushed on to the outskirts of Mœuvres, which was attacked, and, after heavy fighting, captured on the following day. In the German offensive a week later Mœuvres was held at every point, and all attacks repulsed. The Canal du Nord became the theatre of a swaying struggle which lasted far into the night. The bed of the canal was dry, and formed the battle-ground on which the contending elements met and fell; a murderous machine-gun fire was maintained from either bank and bombs were continually being thrown into the struggling mass of soldiery below—all combined to present a spectacle of devilry and destruction hardly to be conceived. The enemy was unable to make any progress in this sector.

Sector 16—Arras

Route

Take the *Cambrai* road from *Arras* and visit *Guémappe* and *Monchy*, then go on north-east to *Roeux*, and proceed north to *Gavrelle* on the *Douai* road. Visit *Oppy* close at hand. Then make your way north-west to *Vimy*, and return to Arras *via* the *Lens* road.

HOTELS

ARRAS

HOTEL DE L'UNIVERS.

> NOTE.—The normal charges are as follows :—
> Breakfast from fr. 3 to 3.50. Lunch or Dinner
> from fr. 10 to 20. Bedroom from fr. 10 to 18. The
> average cost per day is 40 francs, but during July and
> August it is advisable to reckon this as 50 francs.
> There is a tax of 10 per cent. on all first-class hotel
> bills.

Historical Account

The district comprising the city of Arras, and the neighbouring country, has so often reverted from one sovereignty to another that its history has, naturally, become complicated in the extreme. It has successively come under the sway of the Dukes of Normandy, Burgundy, the Counts of Flanders, the Emperor Maximilian, and finally the King of France. It was captured by the French in 1640. The city contains a magnificent Hotel de Ville, with a superb belfry, 240 ft. high, and a splendid peal of bells. Its decoration is in the Gothic style.

Industrial Account

Some oil and dye works are the specially noticeable signs of an industrial development in this region.

Short Account of the Operations

The principal offensive of the Arras sector was that launched on April 9, 1917. This offensive was designed to eliminate the salient created between the rivers Scarpe and Ancre by the enemy's retreat of 1916, and at the same time to definitely embark on that process of attrition which was henceforth to be so closely pursued by the Allied armies. A subordinate intention was the capture of the height of Vimy Ridge, which would deprive the enemy of valuable observation, and give us the inestimable advantage of a wide view over the Douai plain. The Messines-Wyschaete Ridge was also to be attacked. Within forty minutes from the opening of battle the whole of the German front line system was in our hands. Against the second lines sterner resistance was encountered and our advance slowed down. Nevertheless, by midday the whole of the second objectives were in our possession. Vimy Ridge was captured by 1 p.m., the Canadians having accomplished their task with great bravery. Up to this time the weather, always one of the decisive factors, had remained fine, but on the evening of the first day it definitely broke. Thereafter it became stormy, with violent squalls of wind and rain, and falls of snow. These conditions imposed great hardships on the troops, and seriously hampered operations. Delay was inevitably the result in all quarters— in the movement of guns, the conversion of defence systems, relief of troops and other sources of supply and communication. Despite this inclemency, our troops set to work to consummate their gains. On April 10 the capture of the enemy's third line was completed and attempts made to prosecute this success, but lack of co-ordination with the guns impeded the advance. Further progress was made on the 11th, and the important village of Monchy-le-Preux was taken in the course of an obstinate struggle. On the following day, it having been rendered possible for artillery co-operation to be secured, our offensive was resumed. The attacks against Heninel and Wancourt were renewed, and with complete success, both villages being carried, as well as the last defences of the Hindenburg line. The capture of Vimy Ridge, and its instant consolidation, compelled the enemy to abandon all contemplation of counter-action and withdraw from those areas directly menaced by its dominating position. This retirement commenced on April 13, and our patrols were very active in consequence, keeping in close contact with the retreating troops. Many villages fell into our hands, notably Bailleul and Givenchy. Strong counter-attacks against Monchy-le-Preux were all repulsed. Our offensive at this time, though it had gained all its objectives, was persisted in, mainly in order to assist our Allies, the French. For a week, therefore, our labour was confined to organisation and preparation for an early resumption. The weather was now improving and all seemed favourable for the next blow. On April 25, a week after the French offensive had been launched on the Aisne, we attacked on a 9-mile front. Good progress was made at all points. During the afternoon the enemy delivered many counter-attacks, which were pressed with the greatest determination, regardless of loss. In most instances they were repulsed, but on our right we were ultimately obliged by weight of numbers to relinquish our position on the Cherisy Ridge and in the village of Guémappe. In the North, the German Commander made desperate attempts to retake Gavrelle. Five times on the 23rd, and thrice on the 24th, his troops advanced to the attack, but all to no purpose. Later in the evening of the 23rd Guémappe was recaptured. In these operations we took 3,000 prisoners and some guns.

It was now arranged that, as a complement and help to the French movement in the Aisne sector, our armies should continue their attacks on the Arras front until such time as the results of the French offensive had become apparent. Many minor and subsidiary " pushes " were therefore accomplished by the British in the next few weeks, and a number of villages captured ; among others, Arleux-Gobelle, Cherisy village, Rœux, and Tresnoy, the latter of which was assaulted by the Canadian battalions. At the end of the month our Armies had taken, in the course of fighting round Arras, 20,000 prisoners and 275 heavy guns, and had occupied some 60 square miles of territory.

War Facts

MONCHY-LE-PREUX.—This important village, which lies on a commanding hill above the main Arras-Cambrai road, was a source of great anxiety to our troops on the first day of our offensive of April 9. The place was strongly entrenched, surrounded by wire, which, owing to the difficulty of bringing up guns, was still imperfectly cut, and defended with determination for many days. On April 11, in the course of a driving snowstorm, our men gained the village by assault. On the 12th, a further attempt was made to extend our success on the flanks. Both attacks were met with a murderous machine-gun fire, and the enemy immediately put down a terrific barrage in rear of our troops, which practically cut them off from all access and assistance. The result was that two battalions engaged in the storm found themselves isolated in the German trenches which they had just taken, and in the end compelled to hold up the German counter-attacks which were being launched. These two battalions shattered several considerable enemy efforts and held on to their ground, which covered the village of Monchy, to the very last, suffering tremendous losses. They took the edge off the enemy's effort, though at a cost to themselves of practical annihilation. Of some companies not a single man returned, and Colonel Forbes Robertson, with the Brigade Head-quarter Staff, did fine work with a machine gun on the outskirts of Monchy, and effectually prevented the enemy gaining any foothold. The men composing these battalions were of the Newfoundland and Essex units, and it is no exaggeration to say that, by their heroic resistance, a disaster to our plans which would perhaps have been fatal was avoided. The village and height afterwards remained permanently in our occupation.

GUÉMAPPE.—In our offensive of April 23, following the French attack on the Aisne, Guémappe was one of the principal objectives, and the scene of the most desperate fighting. The village stands on the south side of the Arras-Cambrai road, and directly facing the adjacent village of Monchy on the other side of the road. It was captured in our first rush, but at mid-day and during the afternoon heavy counter-attacks developed against it, and, pushed with great determination, regardless of loss, forced us to retire from the village. Later in the evening Guémappe was retaken by the Scots and, despite all the enemy's concentrated blows, definitely retained. The losses of the Germans this day in the region of Guémappe alone were so heavy that a partial paralysis ensued, and our men were suffered for some time to remain in occupation unmolested.

GAVRELLE.—At the same hour and date as Guémappe, the assault of Gavrelle was also undertaken, and with the same success. The village, which was part of the German third line defences, was stormed by two detachments of the Royal Naval Division, and held inviolably against constant counter-attacks during the strenuous time which followed. An artillery officer vouches for the statement that our guns having observed a gathering of 2,000 Germans in a hollow, turned on them such a concentrated fire that they were shot to pieces, not one escaping. Gavrelle was assaulted by the Germans on April 28 no less than seven times, but with no effect. On May 3, however, a successful enemy attack on the troops to the left drove them back, and exposed the flank of the two battalions of West Yorkshires garrisoning Gavrelle. The situation then became very critical, especially as the windmill which overlooked the village had been taken by the enemy. The colonel of the West Yorks took sixty men of his battalion, and held the east side of the village all day against repeated attacks. A company of the Durham Regiment under Lieut. Hitchings, was ordered to retake the windmill, and succeeded in doing so, but were eventually driven out by the concentrated fire of the Germans. They re-formed, and again assaulted, and captured it, only to be ejected for the third time. Once more they reacted, and this time they repulsed the German counter-attacks which ensued, and clung on with immovable obstinacy. Out of their whole strength, one hundred men, sixty had fallen in the struggle, but, as is usual on such occasions, our object was achieved and the beaten enemy discontinued his attempts. Gavrelle was thus relieved in some measure of a menace which, had it any longer threatened, would have compelled evacuation, and the front, as a whole, was heartened and encouraged by the glorious news of the incident.

OPPY.—When Oppy was attacked as an objective of our offensive of April 23 a strong resistance was encountered, and the enemy threw battalion after battalion in ever-increasing numbers against the troops engaged in capturing the village. Supported by a heavy weight of artillery, these efforts were not negligible, and it was obvious that the enemy was desperately determined to prevent any continued advance. During the confused fighting which ensued, two companies, respectively of the 1st Middlesex and the 2nd Argyll and Sutherland Highlanders, were isolated in an advanced position previously abandoned by us, and they remained there for fifteen hours repulsing every enemy swing in their direction, viewing with apprehension the body of the German attack sweeping past on either side. Notwithstanding the apparent hopelessness of their position, they refused to despair, and opposed a stern and protracted resistance to all the successive enemy waves sent out to overwhelm them. In the morning the survivors were discovered, still untaken, in the course of our counter-attack, and the leaders of each battalion received the V.C. for their splendid conduct. The Oppy position was one of the key points in the German lines, and was the goal of many of our most gallant actions. On May 3 two divisions were launched to the assault of this place, but, owing to the darkness in which the operation commenced, some units lost their way and others became confused—finally, after a whole day of sustained combats, we were forced to acknowledge failure. During a strong German counter on this day, Lieut. Harrison, of the East Yorks Regiment, attacked and captured a machine-gun post single-handed and armed only with his revolver, for which deed of conspicuous gallantry he was awarded the Victoria Cross.

VIMY RIDGE and **HILL 145.**—This dominating chain of heights had for long been a sharp thorn in the side of our armies before the Canadian troops, on April 9, rushed the position. By one o'clock on the afternoon of that day, the entire system was in our hands, with the sole exception of Hill 145, in whose dug-outs, tunnels, and subterranean caverns sharp fighting was still in progress. The enemy delivered several counter-attacks from the shelter of these places, and the affair was so complicated that it was decided to postpone further attacks until next day. On the following day the capture was completed, and Hill 145 taken by storm. But many incidents of extraordinary courage occurred during the clearing up of the underground channels at Hill 145. In one instance, it is recorded that four Canadians, headed by Major Macdowell, encountered seventy-two Germans in hiding, and by a piece of audacious bluff persuaded them to lay down their arms and surrender. For this fine piece of work the Victoria Cross was given to Major Macdowell.

RŒUX.—On April 12 the first attack upon Rœux was launched and led to desperate fighting for the possession of the village, particularly the chemical works, around which fiercely-contested point the struggle was prolonged for several days with the utmost obstinacy exhibited on either side. Rœux was devastated by the British fire, and South African troops once more advanced to the assault, but, after enduring heavy losses on their débouchement from Fampoux, the attack wanted weight, and was repulsed by the enemy. 700 yards of open ground had to be traversed between the two villages, and it was swept by bullets. Further efforts were made to get into Rœux on the 23rd, but, under the shattering fire of the German artillery, they collapsed, and a German counter-attack once again pushed us back to Fampoux. On the 28th more men were thrown in on our

side, and launched against the chemical works, but to no purpose.
The German position in and around Rœux was always fatal to our
advances south of the Scarpe river, as their guns enfiladed our lines.
Another attempt was made during the night without success. On
May 3 our troops gained an insecure foothold near the chemical works,
and even penetrated the village, but after desperate efforts to retain
their gains they were thrown out, the Somersets and Seaforth Highlanders especially suffering severe losses. Finally, on May 10, the
whole position was taken at one bound, this being the ninth successive
time that it had been assaulted. Brigadier-General Carton de Wiart,
leading his stormers, entered the village itself. The place was defended
by the Brandenburgers, who were nearly all killed. Two subsequent
German counter-attacks were smashed.

||||||||||||||||||||||||||||||||||||||||||||||||||||||||||||||||||||||||||||||||||||||||||||||||||||||||||||||

Sector 17—Ypres

Route

To include *Armentières* at the southern extremity and *Forest of Houthulst* northern end, also *Neuve Chapelle, Ploegstraet, Messines, Wytschaete, Zwartelen, Hooge, Hollebeke, Gheluvelt, St. Julien, Langemarck, Pilken, Poelcappelle, Passchendaele.*

HOTELS

OSTEND
MAJESTIC PALACE HOTEL.

DUNKIRK
HOTEL DU CHAPEAU ROUGE.

BOULOGNE
HOTEL DU PAVILLON IMPERIAL.

LILLE
ROYAL HOTEL.

BETHUNE
PAON D'OR.

YPRES
HOTEL SPLENDIDE.

POPERINGHE
SKINDLE'S HOTEL.

NOTE.—The normal charges are as follows :—
Breakfast from fr. 3 to 3.50. Lunch or Dinner
from fr. 10 to 20. Bedroom from fr. 10 to 18. The
average cost per day is 40 francs, but during July and
August it is advisable to reckon this as 50 francs.
There is a tax of 10 per cent. on all first-class hotel
bills.

Historical Account

Ypres is the great British battlefield in Belgium, as the Somme is
in France, and there is probably no town which has suffered so much
from the ravages of war. Its principal claim to artistic distinction,
the noble structure of the Cloth Hall, possessing a façade of over
450 feet, and which took a century to erect, was repeatedly set on fire
and shelled, and now lies an almost total ruin, but a lasting monument
to the bravery and fortitude of its British defenders. The history of

181

||||||||||||||||||||||||||||||||||||||||||||||||||||||||||||||||||||||||||||||||||||||||||||||||||||||||||||||||||||||||||||||||||||||||||||||

Ypres is less tranquil than its artistic reputation, for it was continually a bone of contention between the Flemish princes and the King of France, and its citizens must often have been distracted in their desire to render allegiance to the proper quarter without giving offence to the opposing interest.

Short Account of the Operations

The Ypres salient first came into being during the race for the sea which succeeded the German repulse from Paris and the subsequent advance to the Aisne. By an enormous effort we effected a junction with the French cavalry on the sea line and formed what was in theory an unbroken front, but which in some places consisted of a few outposts and a machine gun. German attention was now thoroughly concentrated on this sector to the exclusion of all else, they having realised that a break through to Calais and the Straits would be in its way as efficient a substitute to the spectacular entrance into Paris as could be found. The British position in front of Ypres was the only obstacle in their path, and they determined that with one immense exertion they would sweep through. The Germans collected some 750,000 troops for this manœuvre, against which we could only oppose a force of less than one-third the number.

The supreme point of the enemy's offensive was reached on October 31, 1914, when all along our front, from Messines to the Menin road, dense masses of men were launched to the attack heralded by a bombardment of unprecedented violence. Short of artillery support and weak in numbers, our indomitable soldiers resisted the onslaught tenaciously, and each unit clung desperately to the strip of ground which it had been allotted to defend. The Kaiser was present at this time to watch his troops make their supreme effort to achieve victory. The struggle was fierce and protracted, and for three weeks the issue was in suspense. On all parts of the front memorable instances of unconquerable courage were conspicuous, and it is sufficient to say that every man behaved as if his own home and family were at stake. The enemy was repulsed at all points, and neither on that day nor any day following could he traverse a mile of that coveted ground which led to Calais. Time after time he renewed the battle, to meet only with a more crushing defeat each time. His losses in this great push must have been crippling, as for many months he remained quiescent.

On June 7, 1917, our first important reaction in this sector was delivered, and from that time onward we gave the enemy no rest. The attack was designed to capture the dominating height known as the Messines-Wytschaete Ridge, and, covered by a concentrated bombardment which overwhelmed the enemy's trenches, our troops swept

Sector 17—Ypres

over his first line defences. Australians and New Zealanders were the divisions mainly concerned. Four hours after the opening, New Zealand contingents had captured Messines, and troops from the North and South of Ireland cleared Wytschaete, fighting side by side. Heavy fighting took place throughout the day in Wytschaete until all the enemy elements were either killed or captured. At 4 o'clock in the afternoon Oostaverne, a village situated on the eastern slopes of the Ridge, had fallen into our hands, and the range and objects of the operation had been reached.

On July 31 a further offensive was launched farther north, the scope of which was much larger, and which was attended by the same degree of success, from Hollebeke in the south to Bixschoote and Houthulst Forest in the north. The resistance of the German infantry was quickly overcome and rapid progress made at all points. All our second objectives were taken according to time-table, with the exception of the stronghold north of Frezenberg, known as Pommern Redoubt. Fighting continued around this place for many hours before it was captured by the West Lancashire Territorials. Later, heavy and obstinate fighting took place on both sides of the Menin road. At the end of the day, our men had already gained the crest of the hills, and had denied the enemy observation over the Ypres plain. On our left, the French, who were actively co-operating, had kept in close touch and had also reached all their objectives. Our subsequent progress was marred by the unfortunate breakdown in the weather, and for four consecutive days it rained incessantly, impeding our consolidation work and preventing any resumption of the battle. The enemy delivered several counter-attacks with the object of dislodging us from our new positions, but with no effect. In August an improvement took place in the weather which permitted a renewal of operations, and on August 16 our second attack was launched east of Ypres, in concert with the French on our left. The important village of Lange-marck was captured after sharp fighting, but in the centre the enemy had constructed, in lieu of deep dug-outs (which would have been subject to constant flooding), strong " pill-boxes " of reinforced con-crete, which were distributed in favourable localities. These small forts offered a serious resistance ; heavily armed as they were with machine-guns and manned by desperate men, many held out all through the day and delayed our advance considerably. Hostile counter-attacks had also to be continually repelled, and a relapse in the weather prevented aeroplane observation being entirely accurate. Our advance, therefore, slowed down a good deal, and at the end of the day our line remained unchanged. Owing to the state of the weather, nothing further was undertaken till September 20, when another offensive was launched east of Ypres on a front of about ten miles, as a result of which the whole of the high ground crossed by the Menin road reverted to our possession, as well as 3,000 prisoners. No less than eleven counter-attacks were successfully resisted. A week later, on September 26, our advance was still further accelerated by

183

the capture of the whole of Polygon Wood and the repulse of several counter-attacks. During the days which followed, more progress was effected, and our position on the Ridge rendered still more secure. In the North, Poelcappelle was captured with 5,000 prisoners. The effect of our advance upon the morale of the German troops was so serious that Ludendorff lays special stress on it.

The next appearance of the Ypres salient is in connection with the German offensive on the Lys River, which unexpectedly developed into a serious move in the direction of the Channel Ports. Following a prolonged bombardment of gas shells on the Lens-Armentières front, the enemy launched his attack on the Portuguese Division round Neuve Chapelle, and broke into the trenches. The area attacked soon spread north and south, and the situation became fraught with danger. Two of the adjoining divisions in line had their wings isolated, and were ompelled to fall back and form a defensive flank ; meanwhile a gap had been opened, and an opportunity offered for success which the enemy was not slow to seize. Our advanced posts held out to the last, and inflicted heavy loss on the Germans, but the impetus of their rush carried them over our lines, and, almost before our plans could be altered, their advanced machine-guns were on the banks of the Lys. After heavy fighting, the crossing at Bac St. Maur was lost, and the enemy, crossing here and at other points, progressed rapidly. Many divisions had now completely lost touch with one another, and were obliged to act entirely independent of a headquarters scheme. Guns were quickly brought up by the enemy, and used to command the passage of the river. During the night he occupied the important bridgehead of Estaires, but a counter-attack of our men regained it. All through the darkness fierce fighting continued in the village for possession of the bridge, and the sway of the battle was continually in doubt. The efforts to capture Estaires were renewed on April 10,1918, this time with better success. In the course of desperate street fighting our troops slowly gave way to the German infantry, and, eventually, after a most gallant resistance, withdrew to the outskirts. East of Messines hostile attacks had also developed, which ended in the enemy effecting a lodgment in our lines from whence he could not be ejected. Heavy pressure was now apparent on all sectors, and in order to keep, as far as possible, in touch with the other units, a retreat was directed. After hard fighting Ploegstraet Village was lost, and our former positions as far as Hollebeke were carried at the same time as he entered Messines. South African units retook Messines on the afternoon of the 10th, but relinquished it again when the evacuation of Armentières (now flooded with gas) compelled an adjustment in that direction. Detachments of German infantry pushed along the Lys canal and entered Merville. In the afternoon of the 11th, the enemy, by a fierce attack, regained Messines, but was unable to issue from the village owing to the steady fire of the South Africans. It was now determined that a general retirement should take place in order to shorten our line and economise men. This was done, and the situation thereafter became more hopeful.

Repeated thrusts of the enemy in the direction of Hazebrouck were vigorously repulsed, though the loss of Bailleul and Neuve Eglise may be said to have counterbalanced the failure. The reinforcements were now in constant transit, and the relief of many battle-scarred units was able to be accomplished with a corresponding gain in efficiency and mobility ; after the withdrawal from Kemmel Hill, all the further attempts of the enemy to press his advantage were useless, and following our great offensive in the south, the evacuation of the Lys salient by the enemy was begun on August 13. Thus ended the cycle of battles for which the name of Ypres will remain distinguished throughout posterity.

War Facts

ESTAIRES.—A large village which lies on the bank of the River Lys, and which was the scene of some of the most desperate fighting of 1918. The enemy's advanced elements reached the outskirts on the afternoon of the opening day, and, having obtained a crossing at Bac St. Maur, further north, swept down upon the division in occupation from both sides. Bitter street fighting took place during the day of April 10, 1918, in which both armies lost heavily. Machine-guns, mounted on the top storeys of houses, did great execution, until the Germans brought up field-guns and knocked them to pieces. The struggle swayed back and forth through the town until nightfall, when the British division concerned withdrew to another position in the rear.

ARMENTIÈRES.—This ancient and old-world town, having been converted into a swamp of gas in the course of the German offensive on the Lys, in April 1918, was abandoned by our troops until the final advance in August, when we re-occupied it.

KEMMEL HILL.—This small, but strategic eminence, entrusted to the French troops, was taken by the enemy troops on April 25, 1918, after much deadly hand-to-hand fighting on the crest. Some gallant French elements held out in a section of the defences on the summit until a late hour after the position had been captured, and thereby rendered a great service to the conduct of the operations.

POLYGON WOOD.—One of the final strongholds of the German resistance in the third Battle of Ypres, 1917. Confused and bloody combats took place for some days in the woods before the whole position was definitely seized. Australians played the major part in the operations in this district, and their deathless bravery gave a tinge of glory to the performance which will never fade. Constant counter-attacks against the wood were repulsed, and a number of prisoners taken.

LANGEMARCK.—This large town on the Ypres-Staden Railway was taken, after a determined resistance, in our attack of August 16, 1917. The operation was carried out in darkness, and needed great skill in assembling the troops to avoid awakening the attention of the garrison. While the assault of the pill-boxes near the Steenbeek stream in this district was in progress, an act of bravery was accomplished so startling in its merit as to deserve special mention. Sergeant Cooper, of the Rifle Brigade, who led a small party against one of these miniature redoubts, had all his comrades shot down, but, without flinching, continued on his way, crossed the bullet-swept ground, and, firing through the loop-hole with a revolver, forced the occupants to surrender. For this act he received the Victoria Cross.

PASSCHENDAELE.—The name given to the ridge and village around whose base the long-drawn-out struggles of May 1917 were enacted. After our advance earlier in the year, it was impossible to allow our armies to tamely submit to the observation throughout the winter which, from the Passchendaele ridge, the enemy was able to exercise. Therefore repeated efforts were made to capture this tiny height, and with it the safety and security our tired armies needed so much. The weather conditions at this season were cold, wet, and unsuitable, yet such was the situation in which our armies were placed that only an offensive movement could free them. By means of slow and regular progress, we gained the slopes of the ridge about the end of October, and on November 6 the Canadians crowned the whole magnificent action by sweeping over the last defences of the village and capturing the position. It was the result of three months' hard and continuous work, advances often made up to the waist in mud, food scarce and uncertain, and death by drowning as likely an end as a German bullet. For patience, endurance, and unalterable determination, Passchendaele will remain for ever fixed in the memory.

GHELUVELT.—A small village on the Menin road, Gheluvelt is celebrated as having witnessed the supreme attempt of the German army, under the eyes of its Kaiser, to break through the British lines to Calais. October 31, 1914, was the date of the action, which commenced with an artillery bombardment of unheard-of violence, lasting eight hours. So many batteries were concentrated on the small area of ground about the Menin road that the position was at last rendered untenable ; dense masses of men being launched against the trenches occupied by the poor survivors. The lost trenches were retaken later by the Worcestershire Regiment in a very gallant charge across 250 yards of ground swept by shrapnel. The village of Gheluvelt, however, remained in German hands.

MESSINES-WYTSCHAETE.—These two villages, with the ridge on which they rest, have been constantly the objects of determined attacks by our army since they passed into the possession of the enemy in 1914. It was during the night counter-attack against Messines, on November 1, 1914, that the London Scottish, the first Territorial regiment in France, received their baptism of fire. In this attack they conducted themselves with the intrepidity and courage of tried warriors, and gained a place in the history of the war which is never likely to be forgotten. In the assault against the trenches outside the village, Corporal Seaton, of the 9th Lancers, performed a very gallant action. With the idea of assisting the successful withdrawal of his regiment, he remained absolutely alone in his trench, working his machine-gun until the Germans were within twenty yards. He then, by the exercise of great coolness and presence of mind, managed to evade capture, and eventually rejoined his unit. He was awarded the Victoria Cross.

In June 1917 the Messines-Wytschaete ridge and the two villages, together with the elaborate systems of defence and communication which the enemy had spent the intervening years in constructing, were carried in one rush by Irish and New Zealand troops, and were not relinquished until the unfortunate affair of the Lys salient in April 1918. At that time, in accordance with the general scheme, it was abandoned temporarily, once again to revert to our arms in October of that year.

GIVENCHY.—One of the few points that sustained with success the German onrush in the Lys salient in April 1918 ; for, notwithstanding the immense masses of men that were continuously launched against the stronghold, its defence works were so well constructed, and its garrison so obstinate, that the combination of the two proved considerable—at least, for the Germans. As the German advance extended to a greater depth, the situation of the troops here became more and more perilous, and they were forced to prolong their line almost to breaking-point to keep in touch with their comrades. Fortunately, no further sacrifices were required of them, and from now, until the days when our final glorious advance to victory commenced, they rested tranquil.

NOTES

NOTES

NOTES

NOTES

NOTES

Milton Keynes UK
Ingram Content Group UK Ltd.
UKHW050859140524
442681UK00007B/160

9 781783 319473